THE FINE ART OF

SMALL-SCALE WOODTURNING

(Photo by Peter Stevens)

William R. Duce

Sterling Publishing Co., Inc.
New York

DEDICATION
To Nancy, without whom none of this would have ever been possible

Library of Congress Cataloging-in-Publication Data
Duce, William R.
       The fine art of small-scale woodturning / by William R. Duce.
          p. cm.
       Includes index.
       ISBN 0-8069-6301-8
       1. Turning. 2. Woodwork. I. Title.
TT22.D83 1999
684'.083—dc21   98-40914
                                                                                    CIP

Project photos and studio shots by Peter Stevens
Other photos by William R. Duce or as credited
Book design by Judy Morgan
Edited by Rodman Neumann

1   3   5   7   9   10   8   6   4   2

Published by Sterling Publishing Company, Inc.
387 Park Avenue South, New York, N.Y. 10016
© 1999 by William R. Duce
Distributed in Canada by Sterling Publishing
c/o Canadian Manda Group, One Atlantic Avenue, Suite 105
Toronto, Ontario, Canada M6K 3E7
Distributed in Great Britain and Europe by Cassell PLC
Wellington House, 125 Strand, London WC2R 0BB, England
Distributed in Australia by Capricorn Link (Australia) Pty Ltd.
P.O. Box 6651, Baulkham Hills, Business Centre, NSW 2153, Australia
Printed in Hong Kong
All rights reserved
Sterling ISBN 0-8069-6301-8

ACKNOWLEDGMENTS

There comes a time in the preparation of any manuscript for the author to tackle the impossible task of thanking everyone who has contributed to their efforts. Looking back on the past year, there are far too many individuals who have assisted me to one degree or another, and I fear that I will omit someone that I shouldn't.

The short list is that I would like to sincerely thank everyone whom I have come in contact with in the past year and a half for their input, whether they realize it or not. That out of the way, there are several people that I would specifically like to recognize. I was originally planning to divide the group between professional and personal contacts, until I realized that all of the professional turners and suppliers I have met have treated me more like a friend than a distant business acquaintance. I can personally vouch for the adage that "turners are the nicest group of people you are ever likely to meet."

When I was researching how to submit a book proposal, it was suggested that the budding author should contact well-known figures in the field and solicit one fo them to write an introduction. "Great," I thought. But the only problem was, I did not personally know any well-known professional turners. Instead, I followed my motto of always trying to start at the top and work your way down (this way, rejection is almost expected and easier to accept). I wrote a letter of introduction to David Ellsworth to inquire if he would be interested in my project. A couple of weeks later, I received an enthusiastic reply that he would indeed, and the rest is history. So for the record, thank you David. Your words of encouragement were a reassuring wind in my sails.

I was quickly to find out, however, that David's response was not unique in the world of turning. Almost without exception, every other turner I approached to submit slides of their work responded with equal enthusiasm. Once again, thank you Mohamed Zakariya, Bill Jones, Craig Lossing, Mike Lee, Hans Weissflog, David Sengel, Kip Christianson, Michael Mode, and Bonnie Klein.

Another individual to whom I am eternally indebted is Kevin Wallace at the del Mano Gallery. I am sure that the wonderful photographs he sent to be included with the proposal went a long way to securing its acceptance. When the time came to contact these individuals, he patiently supplied me with addresses, and phone numbers and, in one instance, he actually forwarded my letter.

My appreciation also goes out to the suppliers who have provided samples of their wares: Dick Lukes, at Beech Street Toolworks, for going above and beyond the call of duty; Brad Packard at Packard Woodworks; Jim Fray at Wild Woods, for explaining the process of stabilization; Donna Long at EZE-LAP Diamond Products; Peter Gill, from Robert Sorby; and Mark Freeman at Mammoth Ivory Co. I am also grateful to Andrew Poynter at A&M Wood Specialty, Inc., for reading over some of the text and making corrections where it was warranted, and to master-pipemaker Mark Tinsky, at the American Smoking Company, for sharing his finishing recipe with the rest of the world. I would also like to mention the photographic wizardry of Peter Stevens, for his skillful handling of the project photos, and for treating the still lifes of my work in a sympathetic manner.

My appreciation goes out to all of the many at STERLING PUBLISHING CO. who have had a hand in the book from conception to distribution. Specifically, Judy Morgan, for the wonderful book design and gallery, and Rodman Neumann for editing and layout—I can only hope that every author should be so fortunate to have as fine an editor as he.

On a personal note, I must thank Greg Rice and his family for tolerating my sometimes weekly trips out to play in their shop. If not for their patience, I doubt whether I would have pursued my interest in the craft.

To my mother, grandmother, sister Deb, and brother Dan and his family, I thank them for always being supportive of my decisions and schemes, even when I was not always sure that I was. While it may not have been a traditional family environment, it was always (usually) nurturing and loving.

My final acknowledgment has to go out to Nancy, and Romasz, Horansky, and Sparks families, for accepting me and assisting in all of my endeavors (even if I do send rude greeting cards). Nancy is my best friend, supportive critic, personal baker . . . and she dances a mean swing.

CONTENTS

Kip Christensen (Photo by Photocraft, Orem, UT)

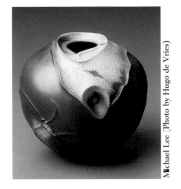

Michael Lee (Photo by Hugo de Vries)

David Sengel (Photo by Michael Siede)

David Ellsworth,
"Two Vessels,"
cocobolo/rosewood
burl, taller 1⅜".

FOREWORD

A PERSPECTIVE ON SMALL OBJECTS

*Never underestimate the power
of small objects in our work.*

PAUL SOLDNER, American ceramic artist

***Hans J. Weissflog,
"Star Box,"
African blackwood,
1⅞" by 2⅞".***

(Photo by Hans J. Weissflog)

 Paul made the above statement to me soon after we first met in Aspen, Colorado, in 1974. Looking back over the years, I now see how prophetic his words have become. In particular, small objects have now begun to gain a level of acceptance within the field of woodturning that is providing an important balance to the larger, more "visible" objects that have come to symbolize woodturning as a viable creative medium within today's contemporary craft movement.

Small turned objects have, of course, been made for centuries and in many cultures. However, what is most interesting about the work being produced today is not only the diversity of the objects themselves, but also the level of acceptance these objects have received as an inclusive part of the studio woodturning movement as a whole.

Equally important, many turned objects that are both contemporary and historic, utilitarian or decorative, are being acknowledged today as legitimate art forms.

As an example: In 1983, the American Craft Museum in New York, mounted an exhibition that was curated by then-director, Paul Smith. Titled "The Art of Woodturning," the content of this exhibition was approximately 30 percent contemporary "decorative" woodturnings and 70 percent "historical" work! The objects from the latter group included functional toys, tools, and implements brought from many countries around the world. Thus Smith's intent was not simply to exhibit work that was currently "hot" in the marketplace, but also to show the breadth of what woodturning is and always has been.

Another measure of the growing credibility of small turned objects is

David Ellsworth. "One Hundred Spirit Forms," tallest 3½".

the frequency with which prominent collectors in America have begun to donate portions of their woodturning collections to major museums throughout the country. Among them: the Renwick Gallery of the Smithsonian Institution, the Los Angeles County Art Museum, the American Craft Museum, the Mint Museum, the Metropolitan Museum of Art, and a dozen others. Many of these pieces are small objects, one in the Metropolitan collection being only 5/8" tall x 3/4" in diameter! These small objects now share equal space and therefore equal credibility with all the other objects in these museum collections.

A logical question: Does this then mean that every small object produced on the lathe is now an "art" object? or that every legitimate hob-byist craftsperson can now hang the hallowed halo of "artist" over his head? Hardly. Art has always been regarded as a balance between the intent of the maker and the acceptance—possibly even the tolerance-of the culture. What it does mean is that the barriers of bias between craft and art have begun to shrink to the point where we can now honor any person's right to express himself creatively, regardless of their intent. Thus the doors are now open to good work on all levels, for it is good work that has opened these doors.

Certainly one of the greatest challenges turners have encountered in making small objects comes in the area of design. Small objects are actually more difficult to design than their larger cousins, simply because any reduction in scale magnifies every nuance of an imperfect curve, an over-rounded edge, or a slightly mismatched glue joint. In fact, turners have often sacrificed the principles of good design by relying instead on the wizardry of micro-techniques or the magnificence of the materials used as a criterion for excellence in their work. One of these principles involves "monumentality." That is, if an object is equally successful at three feet as it is at one inch, it can be considered monumental in its design. If not, it might be considered almost anything, even "cute"; but probably just "small."

Another question: What is it that is so intriguing, so compelling about small objects? Surely it must be more than just the technical virtuosity that's required in their making. Jewelry is small and intricately made, yet we generally appreciate it in terms of a balance between design and the beauty (or cost) of the materials used. Is it, then, that small objects are so disproportionate to the scale of humans that they draw from us unexpected, untapped emotions?

How about the incongruous whimsy of a Del Stubbs goblet that is a mere quarter-inch tall? . . . Or the mystery and illusion of a hollow form that has the appearance of mass, but is virtually weightless due to the thinness of its walls? Maybe it's our desire to challenge the abstract in a concrete world, as in Stephen Paulsen's three-dimensional paintings with archeological themes, and titles like "Three Pre-Classic Vessels and Aerial View of the Site from the Most Recent Dig on Marquard IV"!

Surely it is all of these, including the opportunity to experience these objects on a very personal and individual level. And to his credit, this might well explain Soldner's use of the term "power" in describing the importance of small objects.

—David Ellsworth

Bonnie Klein,
"Threaded Top Box,"
African blackwood,
osage orange.

*William R. Duce,
"Vessel,"
amboyna burl and
African blackwood,
1¾" by 2½".*

(Photo by Peter Stevens)

THE ART OF TURNING WOOD

. . . the lyf so short, the craft so long to lerne.

GEOFFREY CHAUCER

William R. Duce, Closed vessel project; box elder burl with African blackwood, 1¾" by 2½".

(Photo by Peter Stevens)

 A central question is ever before us: What is craft? My interpretation of craft work in modern society is that it is representative of a skillfully hand-made object that has been created for a utilitarian standard. Simply put, it is something that is made to be used.

GALLERY VERSUS CRAFT

Popular craft work no longer carries the prestige that it once held with the mainstream public. The word "craft" has now often become synonymous with glue guns, ribbons, power nailers, or faux anything which, for the most part, is totally lacking in artistic merit. It is not that I have anything against someone pursuing a hobby for their own enjoyment or to keep busy. In fact, I wholeheartedly encourage it. It is simply that the majority of the objects I find at most of the regional craft shows are simply mass produced, with a minimal amount of thought or effort put into their construction. This is assuming, of course, that they were not mass produced in a factory to begin with. If these obviously skilled individuals would just invest a little more energy in developing their own personal expression in their work, they would then have the satisfaction of creating objects that bear their own unique visual signatures. My personal rule of thumb is that the surest way to avoid a poor standard of work is to run as fast and as far as you can from any event that spells either "country" or "craft" with a "k." Skilled production turners, on the other hand, are active craftsmen (or more preferably, artisans) who turn multiples of the same basic objects in an effort to earn a living at their trade (also known as a "jobbing turner"). While a well-made production piece is a joy both to see and to use, most of these will ultimately fall a little shy of the gallery standard of work. Craft objects are wonderful one-of-a-kind creations in their own right, but do not really express the same attitude as a fine-art piece.

The gallery turning is representative of an object that takes the familiar medium of turning and, through a combination of design, technique, and content, elevates it beyond the role of the strictly functional object.

SMALL-SCALE TURNING

Before progressing much further in this work, we should define exactly what a small-scale turning is. The term "small-scale turning" was first suggested by Bonnie Klein, one of the reigning masters of the small-scale turning set. It is used to describe objects that are generally under six inches in size but are not miniatures. A miniature is a scaled-down reproduction of a full-sized object. A small-scale turning, on the other hand, is already full sized and,

Mohamed Zakariya, Malay-style chess set, boxwood and ebony.

(Photo by Samuel Gutterman)

to be complete, does not depend upon any extraneous associations with other objects.

DISCOVERING MY TRUE PASSION

My passion for woodturning has taken a rather circuitous route. Unlike many who turn, I was not introduced to the lathe during high school shop class. In fact, my aversion to the manual arts at that time was so strong that I withdrew from shop after a single class in my freshmen year, thinking it wise to quit while I was ahead. My stepfather was somewhat mechanically inclined, and was of the belief that if it had a motor, then he could fix it—eventually.

It was during seemingly weekly repair sessions that my true mechanical aptitude was first made apparent. My official duties entailed carrying the bucket of tools, holding the flashlight steady or, as relief duty, pulling the cord on the lawnmower/snowmobile or (you fill in the blank) after my older siblings had all had enough. It seems as though we marked the changing of the seasons not by flora around us, but by the type of mechanical contraption that sat out front of our door waiting for the parts to arrive.

Throughout the course of my teen years, this (along with one epiphanous incident where I quickly learned the merits of insuring that the plastic insulator should always

William R. Duce,
three early pieces.
The 6" redwood
burl vase on the left
was one of my very
first turnings.

(Photo by Peter Stevens)

be replaced whenever rewiring a lamp) was basically the extent of my mechanical skills. As I was drifting about as far from the industrial arts as any boy who lived in the country could reach (of course, I did learn the mandatory skills of how to siphon gas . . .), I was beginning to discover that I had a certain aptitude for the fine arts, which blossomed under the steady tutelage of both my family and my teachers.

My academic record throughout my high school years was totally unremarkable. I was one of those students who always manage to coast through school while investing an absolute minimal amount of time in schoolwork. I found that I was always more interested in what I

Michael Lee, "Rock-A-Bye Pod," eucalyptus burl, 5¾" long by 3" wide by 3" high.

(Photo by Hugo de Vries)

David Ellsworth, "Kingwood Vessel," 3½" by 3".

THE DECORATIVE ARTS

The problem that one runs into while determining whether an object is either "fine" or "decorative" in nature is that there are no hard and fast rules governing either one. The contemporary craft market is a mature vehicle that has raised the standards of fine craft work to the extreme limits. At the upper end of the market, the differences between art and craft are all but invisible, which is as it should be. Wood-turning is well ensconced in the world of contemporary craft galleries, and the specialized field of small-scale turning has achieved a great deal of legitimacy among artisans, gallery owners, and collectors alike.

Like most things in life, there are no definitive answers as to what

could learn from the teacher's individual outlook, rather than from any preset curriculum.

After completing high school, I enrolled in a university fine arts program. The first year was great, and offered all that my inquisitive mind desired. But by the middle of the second year, I found my enthusiasm for university life waning to the point that I simply did not bother to return after the Christmas break. Today, I have a hard time identifying exactly where things went awry. I do recognize that one of the main reasons for my discontent was that my at times rebellious (and innate) cynicism kept conflicting with the "ivory tower" mentality that I found to predominate at the university level. The second reason that I left was that I was gradually beginning to realize that my true passions were based not so much in the traditional fine-arts mediums but rather more in the decorative arts.

Craig Lossing,
obony, maplo burl,
bloodwood,
7" high by 12" wide.

(Photo by Craig Lossing)

defines one object as a decorative art object, while a seemingly identical work will be heralded as a wondrous example of fine art. I have always felt that the main difference between the two is that a decorative art object will retain at least a semblance of the practicality upon which the object is based. Fine art, on the other hand, simply exists. It is something you hang on a wall, place on a pedestal, and admire from afar. Fine art is intended to enrich our lives by compelling us to react to it on a higher level.

It has also been my experience that the only true test of any object's relative artistic merits is time. Even the highly esteemed art experts, who spend their lives developing theories and defending their judgments, are often proven wrong by this one great equalizer. To put this theory to the test, all that one has to do is to look at the work from as recently as twenty years ago (fine woodworking design books are good for this). These objects were once viewed by a panel of their creator's peers to be on the cutting edge of design. But

when we look at them today, we often have to stifle a laugh at some of their painfully dated forms. As in so many things, it can be a death knell for an object to link its popularity to a fleeting fad.

Neither the fine-art nor the decorative-art object is inherently superior to the other, and each has its own role to play in our daily lives. If it must be done, then separating the two along imaginary lines is really the job for academics, philosophers, or anyone else who cannot find honest employment. As long as the design of the object projects the integrity of its creator, then I willing-

ly accept both as equals. If it lacks integrity, then it is neither fine art, decorative, nor any other worthwhile aspiration, but simply a visual gimmick.

There has not been a book that approaches the topic of small-scale turning from the perspective of the serious artisan—that is, someone who creates these small objects out of choice rather than as a means of simply using up off-cuts. My objective is to illustrate that bigger is not in fact better and that a finely turned small-scale object is the equal, if not the champion, of its "big-boned cousins."

Most of the techniques of turning are actually quite basic—all that is required to master them is time, patience, and practice. All of this general information can be found in any one of a dozen books written by turners who are far more suited to that particular task than myself. My premise is not so much to offer a "how to" as it is to explain "why to."

The projects are intended to be used as a launching pad for your own development as both a turner and designer. The most important requirement for their successful completion is a basic confidence in your own skills. Once you achieve this, you will be capable of tackling any project regardless of how complicated it may initially appear. None of these projects is exceptionally challenging—I have tried to choose those which will be of interest to both the beginner and the experienced turner.

The Gallery, following the Projects, gives a small sample of some of the small-scale turnings that are currently being created for the contemporary craft market. Here are displayed some extraordinary objects created by a diverse selection of truly gifted artisans, some of whose work is also shown throughout the chapters.

The difference between a small and large turning in the marketplace is usually just one of economics.

There is an erroneous perception that a larger piece is more difficult to turn and therefore commands a higher monetary price. But as the small-scale turning movement continues to blossom, this price differential will keep decreasing.

The question of whether turning is a true art form or simply a craft is a relatively recent conundrum. Historically, only the finest of the ornamental turnings would have been considered to encroach upon the heady world of art and everything else; would have simply been considered craft work. In fact, the life of a typical nineteenth-century turner would have consisted of long hours spent at the lathe, churning out the same job time and time again (it's nice to see that some things never change).

Woodturning was an acceptable avocation for the well-heeled gentleman even before the nineteenth century. The hobby turners of past generations studied the art of the turner for largely the same reasons that you and I practice it today—because they/we enjoy it.

For many turners, this enjoyment that we find in turning has more to do with the actual physical process than it does with any final product. The fact that we may, if all goes according to plan, end up with a completed product at the end of the day is simply an added bonus.

Hans J. Weissflog,
"Double Wall Ball Box,"
African blackwood
and boxwood,
large 3⅛", small 2"

(Photo by Hans J. Weissflog)

2

*William R. Duce,
hollow vessels;
free-form edge,
big leaf maple burl
and African blackwood;
box elder burl with
rosewood accents,
3¼" by 3½" each.*

(Photo by Peter Stevens)

TOOLS OF THE TRADE

Life being very short, and quiet hours of it few, we ought to waste none of them in reading valueless books.

JOHN RUSKIN

"Lidded Container," pink ivory, ebony, bone, elk antler, 3⅝" high by 1⅞" diameter.

(Photos by Photocraft, Orem, UT)

 Whenever I read wood-working articles, I try to look into the background of the photos to see how the artisans have outfitted their shops. I am aware that this kind of behavior may lead to my being labeled as a pathological "tool voyeur," but, luckily for me, I know that I am not alone in this affliction. By "seeing into" the workshop of another artisan, you will be able to glance into his inner sanctum and discern who he is and what type of work he does.

Likewise, the equipment with which you choose to surround your-self will also be an extension of your personal attitude towards your work.

The success of small-scale turning is not inherently dependent upon an extensive selection of tools. Rather than starting out with dozens of tools which you can "kind of" use, you are far better off utilizing only a few which you learn to use well.

I limited myself to three tools during the first year that I did any woodturning: a high-speed steel oval skew at 13mm, a 10mm high-speed steel gouge, and another high-speed steel gouge at 6mm. I found these three generic tools—unhandled—at a wood show, and all that I know of them is that they were made in Sheffield, England, out of high-speed steel. I still find myself reaching for them more frequently than most of the other tools I have since acquired.

For someone freshly starting out, I would have to suggest a few additions to these three tools. One of your better options would be to acquire one of the preassembled tool packages. A basic starter set should include a few gouges, a skew, and a parting tool. The exact size of the tools will be dependent upon the size of your work. If you want to make small bowls, stoppers, and the like, then you will be able to use

Shaping the base of a chess piece with a gouge.

small full-sized tools. If you are interested in turning miniatures and micro objects, then go with a dedicated set of small-scale tools.

There is nothing wrong with using a full-sized tool on a small-scale turning. In fact, I like to take the painter's approach of using as large a brush as I possibly can. Using too small a brush (or gouge) early in the process can result in the artisan becoming overly focused on fine details, when he should really be concerned with the overall balance and composition of the piece.

Although I have stated that small-scale turning does not require a large number of tools, you are probably asking yourself why you have never encountered an experienced turner who does not own racks upon racks of them. The answer (and this is coming from a bona fide chisel-head

himself) is: because we like them. Sure, some of the variants may offer us the opportunity to perform a particular task more effectively than with a standard tool, but for the typical hobbyist the difference is not really all that significant. The trap that many turners fall into is that even though they are quite satisfied with the equipment they are using, upon hearing of a well-known and admired turner's wondrous new signature tool, they rush right out to purchase one, thinking that it will solve all of their turning woes and enable them to turn just as well as the tool's designer. The fact that the designer has spent the last thirty years mastering his art is often forgotten in all of the excitement.

Every year, new and improved tools compete for our turning dollar. Some of these items are truly useful

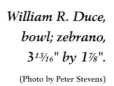

William R. Duce, bowl; zebrano, 3¹³/₁₆" by 1⅞".

(Photo by Peter Stevens)

and a joy to use, while others will quickly end up banished to that corner of the shop that we just never seem to get around to cleaning. The design of some of these so-called new tools is frequently only a rehashing of an old style brought up-to-date. Nineteenth-century turners did not have the luxury of mail-order catalogs that would ship a parcel halfway around the world overnight. If they wanted a new tool, it usually meant that they would either have it made or make it themselves out of whatever materials were available.

Turning has been practiced for hundreds of years, and the same laws of physics have applied throughout all this time. Realizing that most modern turners do not turn as frequently as the professional of the last century, I doubt that we will ever develop a basic new tool that has never before been tried. The only advantages we have over our distant cousins from a few generations ago are the advances made in metallurgy and the related sciences.

The designs by leading contemporary manufacturers like Glaser Industries and Beech Street Tool Works can be attributed to their successful application of contemporary technology to historical designs. These companies have taken a relatively simple principle and refined it with the best that modern technology has to offer. While these tools will generally outperform any of their

Kip Christensen,
"Inlaid Box,"
ebony, leopard jasper,
2⅛" high by
2⅝" diameter.

(Photo by Photocraft, Orem, UT)

historical predecessors (as well as the majority of their contemporary ones), I believe that the hands in which they are held would have a hard time competing against those of the turner of yore.

The Golden Rule, when purchasing any new tool or other piece of equipment, is to always acquire the very best that you can afford. Every woodworker has suffered through the indignity of trying to use a clamp that won't clamp, a saw that won't saw, or an axe that won't axe . . . er, chop; and it is one that is to be avoided at all costs. The pennies that you will initially save by purchasing the cheaper alternative will never be sufficient to cover the costs of replacing the tool with the one that you should have acquired in the first place.

THE SKEW

Skew chisels have developed a bit of a stigma about being difficult to use or for biting the hand that wields them. The reality is that while a skew may be a little more difficult to master than most other tools, once you have it, it will become a sheer joy to use. Rolling beads, performing long smooth planing cuts, making shoulder cuts and more are all in the province of this tool.

When a skew does catch on a turning, it is a frustrating and sometimes angst-ridden experience. With small-scale turning, most of that anxiety is removed since you are working on something measured in inches—not a three-and-a-half-foot-long piece of four-inch hard maple for the leg of a harvest table. Practicing with a skew on a miniature lathe is ideal for anyone with a fear of this tool, as it allows you to get up close and personal with what you are doing. If you do get a catch, the only thing likely to be injured will be your pride.

My enthusiasm for skew chisels is such that I have had one custom-forged by Mike de Punte, of Cape Forge Tools. Mike hand-forged a piece of W-1 steel to the dimensions that I supplied, and then flame-hardened and triple-tempered it to a Rockwell rating of 62 before polishing it to a near-mirror surface. Is this skew really all that much better than a commercial factory piece? To me it

GOUGES

Removing the bulk of the sides with a gouge for the spinning top.

The gouge is the workhorse for most turning applications. It can remove a great deal of material in a short period of time, as well as cut delicate profiles on all manner of work. Available in a wide range of sizes and grinds, the gouge is well suited for everything from cutting a cove in spindle work to hollowing out the end grain in a container.

The profile which I use on all of my gouges is a medium fingernail style, which allows me to do everything from hollowing the interior of bowls and sheer-cutting the exteriors, to forming tiny coves on cribbage counters. This profile works well for me, but there are several others that may be more suitable for your own work. Do not be shy about experimenting with a new grind. If you do not like it, just grind it back to the way it was before you started.

Using the skew to rough out the blank for the lace bobbin project. You could also use a gouge, but I find the skew quicker.

is. When I turn bobbins or other small spindle work, I will use the skew to do as much as I can—including everything from roughing out the blank to making shoulder cuts, rolling beads, and turning tapers. For me, I want to use the best tool available for the job.

The other reason that I ordered the skew from Mike is that I am a collector of antique tools. In my not-always-so-humble opinion, his tool-making efforts resulted in an heirloom-quality instrument that I have no doubt will long outlast me.

SCRAPERS

The scraper used to be the unsung hero of turning tools. Relegated to simple bowl work by the majority of turners, scrapers never received the same following as the gouge or skew. In fact, unless you are into hollowing work, you do not even need a scraper for small-scale turning. But once upon a time not so long ago, a

gentleman seized upon the idea of creating a purely decorative object featuring a proportionately small opening and thin walls (thanks, David). This seemingly simple design became the inspiration for a slew of imitators, and is still going as strong as ever. For hollowing this type of vessel, the scraper has became a tool of necessity.

Today we can find scrapers in all manner of profiles and sizes, from flat to round nose, straight to bent to sheer, and everything in between.

Using a flat scraper to true up the walls and bottom of the ring box.

PARTING TOOLS

As a small-scale turner, there are two parting tools that I would not want to do without. The first is ½₀" wide by 1¼" high and 8" long, and is manufactured by Crown Tools. This is a strong, simple tool that I prefer to use for most of the grunt work. It can be safely extended a fair distance from the tool rest in order to reach into areas inaccessible with other tools.

My second parting tool is the P/S 250 from Beech Street Toolworks. This parting tool is without a doubt the finest small-scale parting tool on the market. The width of the blade is 27 percent thinner than a dime at 0.040", and the complete tool exudes an aura of quality, with a heavy brass ferrule and beautiful cocobolo handle. The true value of this tool is not how it looks but how it performs. On domestic timber, it

Using a parting tool to partially part the blank for the closed vessel project.

cuts without any noticeable resistance, resulting in gossamer-thin shavings. On the harder exotics, it can have a tendency to be a little "grabby." (I have predominantly noticed this with African Blackwood.) What I do to counteract this tendency is engage the turning slightly above the centerline, and then carefully lower the blade and nibble away the waste a little at a time.

CHATTER TOOLS

A chatter tool is a poor man's answer to an ornamental lathe. It consists of nothing more than a thin piece of steel that "chatters" when it is introduced to a revolving blank. This chattering creates a decorative pattern on the surface of the wood that will vary depending upon the speed of the lathe, the force of the application, the speed at which you move the tool, and the profile of the cutter.

The patterns formed by this tool can be very striking as an accent. From a design viewpoint, you must be careful not to overuse the chatter tool. Chattering is wonderful when simply used for an accent on a turning, but I find that it usually comes up a little short when used as the focal point of a work.

MAKING YOUR OWN TOOLS

Making your own tools for small-scale turning is a simple and often necessary endeavor. The economy of

The Bill Jones point tool is a cross between a skew chisel and a scraper. This tool has actually been in existence a lot longer than Mr. Jones has, but he is responsible for renewing its popularity through both his writing and turning.

This tool is extremely user-friendly. The physical mass of the tool all but eliminates any possibility of flexing, and while the handle looks rather crude, it is the most comfortable factory-applied handle I have ever used.

Planing cuts along the grain are a simple matter with the point tool. Perhaps its greatest asset

is in forming beads. In traditional hardwood and ivory turning, beads are formed with a parting tool by starting low and rolling high—which is the direct opposite of the commonly accepted methods with a conven-

tional skew. But hardwood and ivory turners do not constrain themselves with rules, and they are willing to use whatever happens to work best at the moment. I initially had mixed results when I

The Bill Jones point tool is used here to cut any beads, and generally refine the overall shape, in the tool handle project.

tried to form a bead with the point tool, but after a bit of practice (far less than needed with a skew), I now find that it excels at the task.

The last area where I regularly use it is on faceplate turning. I find that this tool is the perfect instrument for sheer-scraping the exterior of small bowls; it is, as well, surprisingly adept at cutting beads into the side grain of the bowl.

scale means that your tools are not going to be subjected to the same stresses as they would with a larger turning and, likewise, that you will be able to utilize materials that would not be suitable for larger-sized turnings.

The easiest and most popular tool to make is the scraper. Basically, all that is required is a proportionate piece of steel that you can grind into the shape you desire. Old files have historically been used for this purpose and are still utilized by many

turners. There are two schools of thought concerning the use of files to make scrapers. One says that they are dangerous and should never be used. The other states that large files are perfectly safe if they are properly used, have been in use for years, and are only likely to break if they come into contact with a revolving chuck. My thoughts: If you are comfortable using them, then by all means go ahead. But if you are at all hesitant, there are lots of alternatives available to use instead.

The Klein Woodturning Lathe is arguably the finest "easily" portable woodturning lathe available. It features a 5" swing, 12" between centers, and has numerous add-ons and accessories (chucks, an indexing system, and—perhaps most interesting of all—a threading jig) available for the enthusiastic turner.

Concrete nails are one of the best materials for miniature scrapers, and have been used for many years by David Ellsworth (at least, he is the first turner I heard of using them). All that you need to do is grind a cutting edge, bend it to any shape you desire, and then mount it in a handle. I have also used old screwdrivers, Allen keys, and just about anything else that I thought I could get away with.

LATHES

The interest in small-scale turning has prompted manufacturers to introduce a diverse selection of small lathes to tempt the tool-buying dollar. Ten years ago choices would have been limited to only a handful.

Today, however, it seems as though there is a new one being introduced on the market every six months.

Before shopping for one of these small-scale lathes, you first should determine what exactly you want it to do. Are you looking for your first lathe, or just something that is easily portable and can be taken on the road with a minimum amount of fuss? Do you want to turn dollhouse miniatures, or do you want something capable of turning vessels up to five inches wide and two or three inches thick?

Besides the fact that not all small lathes are created equal, they are also not all created to do the same things. The main purpose of some of these lathes is for the production turning of pens and the like, while others are actually small metal lathes with woodturning attachments, and yet more are meant to be able to turn at the outer limits of the small-scale range. There is no one lathe that is the best at everything, but there are several that are quite good at whatever (within reason) you may ask of them.

The characteristics that you should look for in a lathe include a high standard of workmanship, accurate construction, and a basic overall solidity. Beyond these basic points, the exact specifications of the unit you are interested in will be governed by what you want to be able to do with it.

My two main criticisms of many of the small lathes on the market is that they do not come equipped to turn at a truly slow speed (200 to 300 rpm), nor do they have an indexing attachment. An indexing attachment is a relatively simple device that would add a minimal cost to the lathe if equipped at the factory. An indexing attachment is simply a device (often a plate attached on the head stock) that is equally divided around its circumference to enable the turner to easily and accurately divide the turning into equal sections.

TURNING SPEED

When I turn, I do not particularly feel a great need for speed. High speeds can be useful at times, but are always secondary to using sharp tools. Before increasing the speed to gain a smoother cut, make sure that your tool is sharp and is not to blame for any problems you may be experiencing.

The latest addition to the line of mid-sized lathes is the Oneway 1015. It features a 10" swing, 15" between centers, a No. 2 Morse taper, and electronically variable speed. This is a much anticipated follow-up to Oneway's full-sized model.

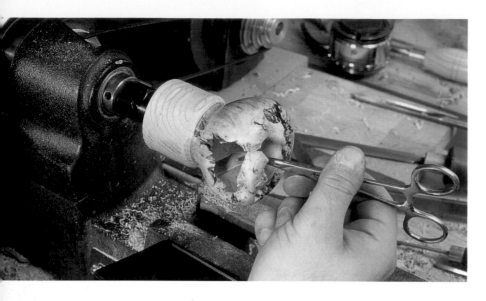

ADDITIONAL EQUIPMENT

I can't remember who originally said, "If you can see it, or if you can feel it, then you should sand it," but I agree one hundred percent. Sanding the interior of natural-edged bowls on the lathe can be a little risky, especially if they have voids like this one. These small locking medical clamps work great, and can be found in both straight and curved models.

As we all know, it takes more than a lathe and tools to turn . . . or does it? Well, yes it does, but how much more depends upon the person and the space? I am restricted by the space in which I have to work and the equipment that I can use. In an ideal world, we would all have a large, airy shop outfitted with one of everything, but in this world that is just not the case.

The only power tools I have—in addition to my lathe—are a grinder/sharpener and a hand drill (not even cordless!). That's it. If I had the room, I would certainly add a band saw, drill press, and stationary sander, in that order.

The hand tools that I regularly use for turning are: various saws (Japanese Dozuki, coping, jeweler's), chisels (both carving and firmer), files and rasps of assorted cuts and sizes, vernier caliper, inside and out-side calipers, machinist's depth gauge, wooden mallets, block plane, drill bits, egg beater drill, awls, and a carving knife and the typical sundry items found in most households (i.e., screwdriver, pliers, and the like).

The Dozuki saw that I use is a utilitarian model that has replaceable blades. Professional Dozukis can be very expensive, are delicate, and are generally unnecessary for our purposes.

There is no doubt that power tools are a great time-saver, but they do not make you turn any better. The most versatile one would have to be the band saw. While most retailers will cut your wood down to size for a nominal charge, having your own band saw is a definite advantage. The only problem with having your wood cut when first purchased is that you may have to live with the wood for a while before you are comfortable with what you want to make out of it.

If, like myself, you do not own a band saw, there are still ways you can get your wood cut to your liking. First of all, as previously mentioned, you could always have the retailer cut it to size for you. If you go this route, I would suggest that you prepare a cardboard cutout of the size you want cut in order to save their time and your money. Also, it is probably a good idea to avoid trying this on a Saturday morning, when most retailers are at their busiest.

The second option is to utilize a friend's saw. Most turners are more than willing to lend a hand to assist you. If you are using a friend's equipment, it is always a good idea to take your host a little extra wood or a saw blade to stay in his or her good graces.

The last option is to use a saw at a local high school. Most schools offer night classes and would not object to your bringing your blanks in to cut up, if you have signed up for a class. There may be other options available to you depending upon your circumstances (i.e., turning clubs, woodworking guilds, etc.) and, if all else fails, there is always the bow saw.

ADHESIVES

Perhaps the only area of woodworking that has progressed faster than metallurgy is adhesives. There are three types of adhesive that I use on a regular basis: PVA, cyanoacrylate, and epoxy.

Polyvinyl acetate glue is the basic standby of most woodworkers. It performs well for the small-scale turner when it is used to laminate pieces, glue a blank to waste block, and anywhere else that you are gluing wood to wood (as long as the wood is not an oily exotic, in which case I will usually use a cyano or epoxy).

Cyanoacrylate, or "Super Glue," is fondly known as the turner's friend. Available in various viscosities, there is one for almost any use. The thick cyano is for gap filling and works well for sealing cracks and doing general gluing jobs. It can also be used to accentuate the crack when is combined with a little dust or a contrasting pigment. The thin stuff will wick into any small crack or joint, preventing it from getting worse. It can also be used to seal your turning before you apply the finish.

Cyano is invaluable to the turner in that it is one of the only glues that will work on green wood. A little cyano goes a long way, and too much can actually impede the bond. A few drops is typically all that most bonds will require. If you use an accelerator with the cyano, keep in mind that the bond is nearly instantaneous, and that you will not have any time to fiddle the pieces after putting them together. The only drawback to the cyanos is that the fumes are strong and they must be used only in well-ventilated areas.

The basic two-part epoxy is an adaptable adhesive that forms a strong chemical bond in most applications. It cannot be used on green wood, but excels at almost all other tasks. I usually prefer it over PVA for attaching unbalanced blanks to a waste block.

Using cyanoacrylate to glue the ebony plug into the top of the box elder vessel, in the closed vessel project.

3

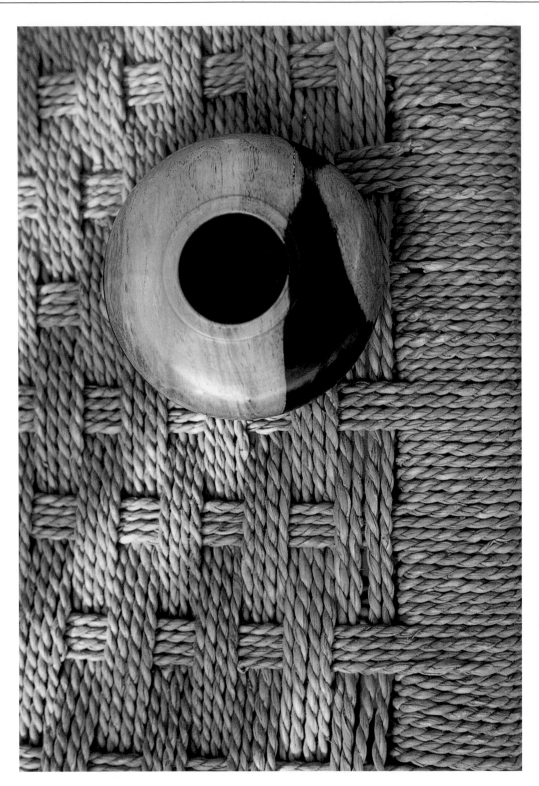

William R. Duce,
African blackwood
hollow vessel, clearly
showing the dilineation
between heartwood
and sapwood,
3¼" by 1¼".

(Photo by Peter Stevens)

THE CUTTING EDGE

Criticism comes easier than craftsmanship.

ZEUXIS, fifth century B.C., from *PLINY THE ELDER*

 I do not plan to add to the reams of paper that have already been written to describe how you should go about sharpening your tools. I do not really care how you sharpen your tools, so long as they are sharp. As any chef or turner can tell you, the necessity of using a sharp tool simply cannot be overstated.

You should never expect a dull tool, not one even moderately dull, to produce a refined turning. The way I think of it is that my goal as a turner has been never to have to use sandpaper to finish a turning. Unfortunately, I am rarely successful at this when turning dried materials (except for boxwood and bone—ah, the pleasures which they give!), but this is my goal. By ensuring that my tools are sharp and my techniques true, I am doing everything I can to fulfill my part of the bargain. The rest is up to the wood. Whenever you make a pass with sandpaper over a turned object, you end up removing it one nth of a degree from where you thought it complete in the first place.

The other reason to always use sharp tools is that a dull tool will require much more force to blunder its way through a cut. If you keep pushing, then I can guarantee that it will only be a matter of time before you eventually overstep the limits of the tool and have either the wood or the tool provide you with a millisecond's worth of adrenal excitement. We must always remember that dull tools are dangerous and impossible to work successfully with. Are you having trouble reproducing the technique you saw one of the pros demonstrate? Hone your tool, try again, and just remember: Pros will never tolerate a dull tool!

For the first year and a half after I started to turn, I used a pair of syn-

Michael D. Mode, "Miniature Chess Set," bubiniga, purpleheart, ebony, holly, Indian rosewood, Tagua nut, 4" diameter by 7½" high (largest vessel).

(Photos by Bob Barrett)

Using a ¼" skew that is properly sharp is the first step in roughing out this blackwood blank for a cribbage counter.

The Lee Valley grinder/sharpener. Basic but effective.

thetic Japanese waterstones to fulfill all my sharpening needs. While these stones, along with a strop, are more than capable of putting a keen edge on any tool, I ultimately grew dissatisfied with the time it took as well as the hassle of picking wayward shavings out of the container of water in which the stones were stored.

For most of us, a power sharpener is clearly the way to go, the only question being: Which one? Your four main options are: a bench grinder fitted with aftermarket wheels; a powered waterstone (either horizontal or vertical); a specialty grinder/sander; or a homemade contraption based on one of the above. Lacking the requisite skills to construct something myself quickly narrowed my choices down. After a great deal of consideration, I went with a belt grinder/sharpener offered from Lee Valley Tools.

This grinder is a simple device that consists of a 1" by 42" belt, which is vertically oriented across a steel platen. In use you simply turn it on—the belt rotates in a downward direction. Either rest the tool on a support or sharpen freehand across the platen, and voilà, you are back in business. One of the reasons I chose this product is that I know from experience that Lee Valley carries a full line of accessories for all the tools they produce. Their selection of 42" belts covers a complete range of the typical sanding grits beginning at 80, and then on up to the nontypical silicon carbide or chromium oxide micro-abrasives in ranges of 15 micron (1000 equivalent), 5 micron (2500), and 0.5 micron (9000), as well as a leather strop.

The other power tools are probably just as effective as the grinder, although their cost is at least double (and then some) as that of the belt sharpener.

Diamond sharpening hones have proven to be one of the better accessories to arrive on the sharpening scene. These handy little abrasives come in a variety of grits, shapes, and sizes and are just the item when you want to touch up an edge for a final pass. Diamond hones are also recommended by several manufacturers for sharpening their scrapers quickly and efficiently. I have found

SEVEN REASONS TO ENSURE YOUR TOOLS ARE SHARP

1. Dull tools are dangerous.
2. Shape with the tool, not with sandpaper.
3. Experienced turners always use sharp tools.
4. Dull tools make you work much harder.
5. Many techniques are only possible with a sharp tool.
6. You heal much faster and with less scarring when you cut yourself with a sharp tool (some-

Cutting the end grain on this hard maple blank requires that your tools are absolutely sharp.

thing I learned in my carving days).
7. Sharp tools not only produce better turnings, but also keep the air you breathe that much cleaner, creating little if any dust.

that once you try them, they will quickly find a preferred spot in your workstation.

One of the old axioms of the turner is that a hollow grind is the best for your tools. While this may perhaps hold true for large work (I doubt it, but I do not turn large work, so I cannot really say), for small-scale objects this piece of folklore is totally off base. First of all, I have a hard time buying into the thought that a hollow grind will assist you in rubbing or "kissing" the bevel of the tool. This would only

hold true if you were turning something that is exactly the same diameter as the wheel with which it was sharpened. Once you extend above or beyond this point, you will have the same amount of bevel in contact with the object as you would with a flat bevel. Even so, it is a moot point. Rather than be concerned over whether or not your bevel is flat or concave, you should just make sure that the tool is as sharp as it can be, and then you will find that everything else will take care of itself.

4

William R. Duce,
ring box;
African blackwood,
1½" by 1¼".

(Photo by Peter Stevens)

YOUR WORKING ENVIRONMENT

The workman ought often to be thinking,
and the thinker often to be working.

JOHN RUSKIN

 When we turn, our time should be spent creating rather then searching for tools, chasing errant accessories, or complaining about our aching backs. Nothing is as important as a comfortable and efficient work environment to help ensure that all our turning experiences are enjoyable.

As small-scale turners, we have a distinct advantage over most other turners because our tools and equipment are, by nature, small and easily portable. When it comes to setting up your own work area, you will first have to determine if it is going to be a dedicated workspace, or if you are going to be forced to pack everything up at the end of each and every session.

TEMPORARY WORKING AREAS

One of the great features of small-scale turning is the portability aspect of miniature lathes. While you do not need a miniature lathe to turn small-scale objects, one will quickly prove indispensable if you do not have the room needed for a permanent work area or if you want something that is easily portable.

A small-scale lathe requires a minimal amount of assembly to prepare for turning. No bolting it to the ground, anchoring it with sandbags, or leveling your floor! A basic arrangement could be as simple as a lathe attached to a piece of plywood that can be easily picked up and moved to wherever it is needed. This is the way I worked for the first eight months that I had my lathe. However, instead of setting the board on top of a table, as any sensible person would, I left it on the floor and developed some quasi yoga-like methods for turning (did I mention that I was living in an apartment?). Eventually I came to

David Sengel, "Box,"
6" high by 3" wide,
cherry, rose thorns,
black lacquer.

(Photos by Michael Siede)

the realization that I was not doing my neck or back any favors, and that it was high time I constructed a workstation that was a little more sympathetic to my complaining bones.

One easy solution is to mount your lathe on a small, 2' by 3' table equipped with casters. Add a few shelves, a magnetic tool rack, power bar, some lighting, and a sharpening system, and you will have everything you will need in one easy-to-move package.

The portable workstation is just the thing for packing up and taking to wood shows, turning clubs, malls, and anywhere else you may be called on to give a demonstration. I have even seen some custom setups designed for the close confines of motor homes and trailers, so that the vagabonds among us can keep their skills in tune while away at the camp site. You may want to consider

A small-scale lathe can simply be attached to a piece of plywood and picked up and moved wherever it is needed. Having a well-organized work area will allow you to complete projects, such as this turned bowl, in the most efficient manner.

designing your workstation with knockdown hardware so that it can be disassembled into smaller components making it easier to handle in and out of your vehicle. Another consideration is to install locks on the cabinet to keep things walking off while you go for a cup of java.

The design of a portable workstation is limited only to your imagination. Be inventive, have some fun, and play around with a variety of designs before you actually put it all together. The possibilities are endless, and you will be amazed at just how much "stuff" you will be able to fit into a small package!

DEDICATED WORK AREAS

A dedicated work area is a nice luxury, but not an essential one for small-scale work. The main difference between a dedicated and a portable area is that with a dedicated space, you have the luxury of not having to pack up and put away all of your toys at the end of the day.

When you are designing a dedicated space, try to keep all of your frequently used tools, chucks, and accessories close at hand. Keep each component stored in its own separate space and make it a habit to return each item to its spot as soon as you have finished using it. Nothing is more frustrating than wasting time searching for a bottle of accelerator that is somewhere in the middle of a mound of turning paraphernalia that you were too lazy to put away in the first place. The less time you spend looking will translate into more time you can spend turning. Of course, having a place for everything and everything in its place applies to temporary work areas as well.

ERGONOMICS

I find that I am more comfortable turning on a small lathe when I am in a seated position. This may not always be possible if you are using a full-sized lathe, but if you can manage it, why not give it a try? A chair allows me to get up close to the turning without being bent over for long periods of time—which in turn will put excessive strain on your back and neck muscles. Preventing neck and back strain will allow you to turn for longer durations at a time and possibly circumvent long-term problems down the road. Remember, it is always easier to avoid a potential problem than to correct one after it has developed (just ask anyone who has ever had a pinched nerve in his or her neck how much fun that is).

STORAGE SPACE

A woodworker can never have too much storage space. The more you turn, the more wood you will end up accumulating. If you are not careful, it is all too easy to find yourself overwhelmed in your own forest of turning stock, off-cuts, and pieces that are just too darn nice to throw

away. As a small-scale turner, I have found this problem to be compounded by the fact that there is no such thing as a piece of wood too small to be turned. If it's a nice piece of wood, then you can be assured you'll eventually find something to make out of it.

There are several ways that you can try to organize your turning stock (which is where most of your storage problems will occur). The method I use will work equally as well in a temporary or permanent space, but is especially appreciated in the temporary area. I store almost all of my wood in stackable plastic storage bins. These little gems are available everywhere, and their versatility is boundless. I have about eight of these on the go, each one categorized by the size and purpose of the wood it holds. The bobbin blanks are in one, round bowl stock in another, burls and such in a third, and so on. Aside from the fact that

You can never have enough storage space.

they are easy to stack, they also help to control the moisture content of the blanks inside.

LIGHTING

Good lighting is an essential element for any style of turning. When you are working within the tight tolerances of a small scale, it quickly becomes mandatory. And, as with the ergonomics of ensuring that you are seated comfortably, good visibility should be secured at all cost. A typical solution for many turners is to attach one or more adjustable draftsman lamps to the tabletop. These lamps are readily available and easily adjusted to almost any angle. If you use two of them, you will be able to use one for the exterior of your container and the second to illuminate the interior of the work.

I use a lamp that has a combination of halogen and tungsten bulbs. The two lights help to neutralize the color that each projects. One word of warning for something I happened to discover the hard way: Make sure to move the lamps out of the way when you are applying a finish to a spinning object—in the event that some of the finish is thrown off and connects with the heated bulbs. The resulting bang and falling glass can be a little unnerving the first couple of times it happens.

DUST COLLECTION

The first solution for wood dust control is to use what I consider to be a basic measure—sharp tools. Sharp tools will cut the wood and generate shavings, whereas dull tools abrade the wood to generate a mixture of large- and small-sized particles. By keeping your tools as sharp as possible, not only will you produce better

Getting light where you need it can be the key to succesfully executing your project, especially in a situation where you need to see inside the end of a piece, as in hollowing out the sides of this toothpick holder.

DANGERS OF WOOD DUST

The dangers of wood dust to the hobbyist woodworker should be a concern for every turner.

How many turners have either said, or heard someone else remark about, how much they love the smell of freshly cut wood? I still do love this smell, and it is this fragrance that I associate with walking into a wood show. However, because of our increasing awareness of the damage caused by dust, as well as by the additional varieties of wood now readily available, we no longer have any choice but to take a proactive stance in the protection of our health.

The Fein 95513 Dust Extractor is an exception to the rule that all dust vacuums are noisy. Because it projects a very tolerable 59.8 dB at 3.5 feet, I have found it to be a welcome change from the previous cheap vacuum that I used, which would wail like a "banshee in heat." It comes standard with a fabric boot that will extract dust down to the 5-micron size. Cartridge filters are available that will filter down to 1.0 micron, or 0.3 with a HEPA filter.

turnings, but you will also keep the air you breathe that much cleaner. Another option would be to turn green wood, which results in little if any dust being generated.

Unfortunately, no matter how careful I am in applying my sharpened tools to the wood, I still find I will usually have to use sandpaper to complete the work. The dust generated by sanding is precisely the stuff

we want to do everything we can to remove from the air. To do this, there are three systems we can use singly—or preferably, in tandem with one another.

The first and most inexpensive method is to use a shop vacuum. The pros to this are that they have a relatively strong suction, good portability, a useful range of attachments to increase their efficiency, and they are widely available. The points against their use are that most of them are uncomfortably loud, you have to purchase additional attachments to help filter out small dust particulate, most are not made to run continuously, and they can generate a wicked static charge that is just waiting for you to reach over to shut them off. If your vacuum does not come with a fine filter already built in, one accessory that is absolutely necessary is an auxiliary filter attachment. In some cases these can be available from the manufacturer, but good ones are also available through many mail-order suppliers.

The next step up for dust collection, and one that I would suggest for anyone in a dedicated workspace, is the traditional style of dust collector. The requirements for small-scale turning are really quite nominal, so any one of the different varieties available should work well (single stage, two stage, cyclone). If you purchase this style of collector, you should do so keeping in mind any other types of woodworking that you might plan to do. The only other thing to be mindful of is whether a fine filter bag is available to fit your collector (something that will work on particles in the 3-micron to 5-micron size).

A recent development from Penn State Industries is this dedicated dust hood that has been especially designed for miniature lathes.

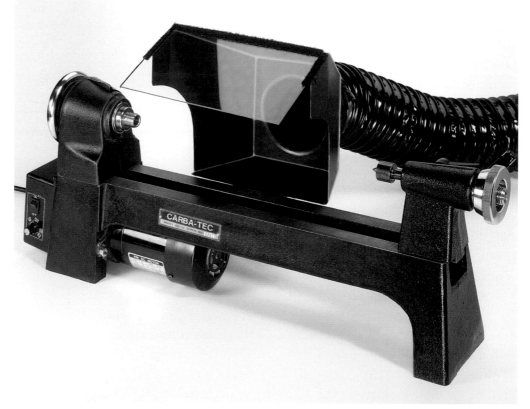

Using the Veritas Magnetic Dust Shoot from Lee Valley to capture the dust from sanding. I really like the magnetic feature of this hood, as it allows me to instantaneously move it to where it is needed.

The third collector is a passive system that you hang from the ceiling. This type continually cycles the air in your shop through a graduated system of filters to remove the airborne particles. I am really quite fond of these systems and would recommend them to anyone as an ideal secondary system to enhance either one of the other controls.

5

David Sengel,
"Box," 6" high by 4"
wide, mulberry, rose,
and locust thorns,
black lacquer.

(Photo by Michael Siede)

A PASSION FOR WOOD

*If you want a Golden Rule that will fit everybody, this is it:
Have nothing in your houses that you do not know to be useful,
or believe to be beautiful!*

WILLIAM MORRIS

 I have to admit that my passion for wood may at times appear a little extreme. There is a certain indefinable quality about working with this once-living material that brings joy to both the young and old alike. While I cannot in good faith propagate that old wives' tale about a finished piece of wood actually "breathing," I do nevertheless believe that a finely finished piece of timber will have retained a little of the tree's soul from whence it originated. There is no other woodworking discipline that can quite compete with the magic of the lathe to release the wood's character. I find carving and cabinetry to be entertaining diversions, but neither is as sympathetic to the inherent beauty of the wood as turning.

The proliferation of specialty wood retailers sprung up across the land has effectively spoiled the modern-day turner. Species that were once a struggle to find are now often only a phone call away. The variety that many of these retailers stock is truly outstanding. I am fortunate in that I live within an easy half-hour drive from two superb suppliers. The larger of the two, A&M Wood, is a well-established international company that normally stocks well over eighty individual species of wood, as well as the numerous subspecies found in each family. This means that if you were to turn only a couple of times each week, there would still be more than enough varieties so that you would never have to turn the same type twice in a single year.

For the hard-to-find imports, burls, and extra-thick stock, these suppliers are certainly the route to take. But when it comes to shopping for domestic species, my preferred source is a local business operated by

*William R. Duce,
"Newton's
Balancing Vessel,"
African blackwood,
tagua nut, abalone,
2" high by
1¼" diameter.*

(Photo by Peter Stevens)

Guy Mechan's Woodhaven is typical of this breed of independent retailer. All of the lumber that is stocked is indigenous to the area, including all of the species one would expect to find (walnut, cherry, maple, etc.), as well as many uncommon, noncommercial varieties (Chinese Elm, pear, mulberry, etc.).

one man with a chain saw and portable bandsaw mill. Odds are that if you were to search hard enough, you would be able to find someone like this in your neck of the woods as well.

These businesses have typically evolved out of the proprietors' own passion for working and collecting wood. Over time, their accumulation of timber surpasses their personal needs, and thus converts itself into a business. The role that these individuals play in the international market is insignificant, but for the small-scale turner they are an incredibly valuable resource for the uncom-

mon, unique, and non-commercial domestic species.

However, even with these two separate sources offering me more varieties of wood than I could ever have the right to ask for, I still find that "the wood always appears to be greener on the other side of the fence." This condition is in part caused by my enthusiasm for experimenting with new and different varieties of timber. I feel a certain excitement whenever I have the opportunity to turn a new species of wood. The promise of the unknown is a beguiling quality that any untried timber holds for the turner.

LOCAL, INDEPENDENT, SPECIALTY WOOD RETAILERS

Who better to purchase lumber from than a fellow turner? While commercial mills will usually cut for yield, you can be assured that a fellow turner will cut for figure.

The small business enterprise of Woodhaven grew out of Guy Mechan's desire to acquire inexpensive timber for his own personal use. Being a self-admitted scrounger, he took only a bit of time before making the acquaintance of the local tree surgeons, sawyers, and public works employees who would assist him in fulfilling his yen for an inexpensive supply of wood. For a time, this was the perfect arrangement. But then one day, as Guy realized that his woodpile was expanding far faster than he could ever hope to have the time to turn, he concluded that his only course of action was to share his good fortune with other woodworkers by selling some of it to them. One thing quickly led to another, and a business was born.

Woodhaven is typical of this breed of independent retailer in that it is run by an individual who is also an end-user of the product. All of the lumber that is stocked is indigenous to the area, some of the lumber will come directly from a mill, other woods have been gathered from development sites, storm damaged trees, orchards, or anywhere that someone has a tree they wish

Guy Mechan's Woodhaven is typical of local, independent, specialty wood retailers.

including all of the species one would expect to find (walnut, cherry, maple, etc.), as well as many uncommon, non-commercial varieties (Chinese Elm, pear, mulberry, and others that can only be guessed at). The source of this wood is unreliable at best. While removed. The fascinating quality about Guy and his ilk is that you never know what you will find from one week to the next, and I doubt if he does either.

It will always be to your benefit to try to befriend these individuals (some would suggest "characters"). Not only will this result in their notifying you whenever they get something a little special in stock but, if you are really lucky, they may even allow you to select and liberate a few choice pieces from their own personal wood cache.

EXOTIC SPECIES

Exotic wood is often synonymous with those dense, tropical species that originate in the rain forest. Typically hard, heavy, and brilliantly colored, these woods have always been favorites of turners. While many of these woods can still be found in a turner's inventory (myself included), concern regarding their use has increased in the last couple of decades. Many turners are now hesitant to use them, due to an uneasiness about the environmental baggage which they carry.

Perhaps the most difficult thing to do, when reaching a consensus of whether or not we should be using these tropical timbers, is wading through all the misinformation and biased viewpoints that have been presented by the mainstream media. The issue is far too complex to be fully resolved in this single forum and, at the end of the day when everything is said and done, the individual artisan is still going to have to make up his or her own mind on whether to feature exotic wood in their work.

WORKABILITY

The working characteristics of the different exotics vary almost as much as the pronunciation of their names. In general, most of the species which I have tried respond

Mohamed Zakariya, "Directoire-style Chess Set," boxwood, boxwood stained black.

(Photo by Samuel Gutterman)

PERSONAL OBSERVATIONS ON EXOTICS

These are a few of the exotics with which I have had the pleasure to work. The comments I have made are simply my personal reflections about the wood, and may not necessarily support those which you have experienced.

The working characteristics of many of the exotics can vary widely between similar species, as well as between separate samples of the same

wood from different trees. The only accurate means of judging how they will behave for you is turning them for yourself.

William R. Duce, ring boxes; African blackwood, boxwood, both 1½" by 1¼".

(Photo by Peter Stevens)

---

favorably to the careful application of a sharp tool. The only real problems I have experienced are that the grain on a few of the species has a tendency to tear out in spindle work and that the dust from some can be a serious irritant. Of the two, the dust is by far the larger concern, for even a slight exposure from certain species can cause an acute allergic reaction in some, and the long-term exposure to any wood dust can lead to severe health problems.

African Blackwood

Near the top of my list of all-time personal favorites is blackwood. It is an extremely dense timber, but generally not quite as black as the

ebonies. Blackwood is the epitome of an "exotic," and it can be finished to a high degree of polish with nothing more than a paste wax. It excels at all tasks on the lathe, but I have found that it can be prone to splintering when carved. The top grade of blackwood is musical instrument quality, meaning that it is free of voids, has straight grain, and has no trace of sapwood or other defects. I find that blackwood seconds turn quite well on the lathe, and in fact are the only grade I will normally purchase. You can expect to find voids, inclusions, and contrasting sapwood in this lot—which, to my mind, only adds to the visual interest of the turning.

Bonnie Klein, "Baseball Bat Necklace," African blackwood and beads.

EXOTICS: TO TURN OR NOT TO TURN, THAT IS THE QUESTION

Whether or not we should be working with these exotic timbers is a difficult question which, unfortunately, has no cut-and-dried solution. More important, I believe that the question we should be asking is: "What is the actual environmental impact of our using these timbers in our small-scale turning?" The consensus that I have received from those

David Ellsworth, "Salt & Pepper Shakers," cocobolo/rosewood, 2¾".

who are intimately familiar with this dilemma is that the impact caused by the serious hobbyist woodworker is basically nil.

To understand this statement—especially after walking into a retailer and seeing stacks of lumber that reach up to the ceiling—we first must recognize that only a very minute quantity of the forests that have been leveled will ever find its way onto the consumer market.

The largest portion of the forest's consumption is attributable to the slash-and-burn practices of land-clearing farmers. This is by far the most criminal use of the land, for the soil is ill equipped to maintain any crop or herd for more than a couple of years—at which

point the process will repeat itself. The ultimate effects of this practice are that it results in decreased wildlife habitat, the sapping of soil for future use, the destruction of a viable renewable resource, the elimination of any possibility for alternative financial gains (i.e., eco-tourism), and the creation of an obscene amount of air

pollution that is an immediate concern for those in the near- and not-so-near vicinity.

Out of all of the hardwood that is harvested worldwide, approximately 25 percent of it is used for shipping crates and pallets. The belief that the forests are disappearing due to over-logging is somewhat misdirected, as the majority of the logging companies are interested in sustaining the resource if for no other reason than that it will ensure their own long-term profitability. While there are certainly some logging companies that poach wood and act unethically, they are in the minority and are as

much an enemy of reputable foresters as the environmentalists.

For the small-scale turner, the economy of the scale of our work affords our conscience some leeway in that we obviously do not use large quantities of wood. The size limitation means that we can often utilize seconds, off-cuts, and other pieces that are left over from other uses.

In many instances, purchasing exotic timber can actually lead to the conservation of the forests by providing a sustainable economic base to a depressed local economy. The question is not one of whether we should use these woods, but more one of whom do we purchase it from. There are currently organizations that inspect and certify both loggers and forests as "well managed," meaning that they practice sustainable forestry techniques to ensure the longevity of the forests. The costs of timber from a certified source may be a more, but can we really afford not to pay it?

Boxwood

Boxwood is perhaps the finest wood to work on the lathe. This wood responds exceptionally well to a skew. Boxwood has traditionally been the favorite of instrument makers, ornamental turners, and anyone else who demands the utmost from wood. You will rarely ever need to sand nice boxwood, and it is capable of holding extraordinary detail when carved. The only problem with boxwood is that, like many of the exotics (although boxwood is *not* a tropical species), it is becoming increasingly difficult to find quality pieces.

Cocobolo

Cocobolo is often used as a substitute when Brazilian rosewood can not be obtained. This is actually a bit of an injustice to the cocobolo since it is a very fine timber in its own right. It responds favorably on the lathe, and is a dramatic timber once finished.

Ebony

There are several separate species of ebony available, but one of the things that they all have in common is that they are all very expensive. One can only expect the prices to continue to increase as the demand exceeds the supply. Ebony turns very well on the lathe, and I find it superior to African blackwood for carving.

Mohamed Zakariya "Short Vessel," boxwood, 7¾".

(Photos by Samuel Gutterman)

Leadwood

Leadwood, as the name would suggest, is extremely heavy and dense. It turns well on a faceplate and is capable of holding fine detail. My limited experience with this wood between centers has been nothing but frustrating. This has been due to the grain running out along the length of the spindle—which has resulted in the grain tearing out. Like most of the exotics, however, once you have it completed, it can be polished to an exceptionally high sheen.

Olivewood

I have always had a love/hate relationship with olivewood. It turns wonderfully and has beautiful grain, but I find that it is prone to checking as it dries. Also it has been my experience that the erratic grain, at least on the samples I have used, were prone to tearing out (of course, not so much that I did not continue to use them). Freshly turned pieces emit a pleasantly spicy smell.

Finishing the exterior of a zebrano bowl before remounting it to turn the interior.

Paduak

One of the more common exotics, paduak is favored for its bright reddish-orange coloring and easy working characteristics. Like some of the other exotics, the coloring of paduak will darken over time.

Purpleheart

There is certainly nothing subtle about the color of this wood. Hard, heavy, and readily available, it turns reasonable well, but you can expect it to darken after finishing.

Rosewood

Like many exotics, the name rosewood can be a catchall for several individual species. The classic Brazilian rosewood (*Dalbergia nigra*) is now only rarely offered for sale, because it has been subject to an importation ban since 1992 under the CITES (Convention on

William R. Duce, toothpick holders; apple, 2¾" by 1¾"; ziricote, 3¼" by 1¾".

(Photo by Peter Stevens)

International Trade in Endangered Species of wild fauna and flora) Act. There does seem to be a limited supply that trickles onto the market from time to time, but one must be cautious that it is indeed pre-ban stock and not poached timber. Brazilian rosewood is a beautiful wood that, if you can find it and are willing to pay a king's ransom for the privilege, is a joy to turn.

Tulipwood

Tulipwood is one of the few light-colored tropical timbers. A near-cousin of rosewood, it shares the same basic grain pattern, only is a soft pink in color. It is truly a fine timber to work and has exceptional color.

Zebrano

Also known as zebrawood, this distinctive timber can be identified from across the room. A yellowish tan color interspersed with deep brown strips, it is one of the coarser of the exotics, but readily available in thick sizes. It works well on a faceplate, but can be a little prone to splintering between centers.

Ziricote

This is a chocolate-colored wood whose distinctively darker pattern lines make it stand out from the crowd. It turns well in all orientations, and I have found it to be a surprisingly decent wood to carve, at least as far as exotics go.

These storage shelves, seen earlier, actually contain a treasure trove of interesting domestics from Guy Mechan's personal horde at Woodhaven.

DOMESTICS

The domestic species which you turn will obviously depend upon where exactly you live. I am surrounded by the typical variety of boreal hardwoods such as maple, oak, walnut, cherry, poplar, birch, and the like. You may personally count mesquite as a domestic, and also perhaps myrtle, redwood, or brown oak and laburnum, or—if you really want to make me envious—koa and mango.

The species that are commonly available are likely to be what you will find yourself turning to most frequently. While we all may have affairs with the exotics, we carry on long-term relationships with our domestics.

Figured Wood

I have yet to meet a turner who does not like to use "figured wood"—which, for simplicity, includes all curly, mottled, beeswing, bird's-eye, quilted, tiger stripe, and so forth, since many erroneously attach these labels to wood that is anything but. Confusing curly maple with curly birch may be understandable. But whenever I hear someone who claims to know what they are talking about call the ray fleck figuring on quarter-sawn oak or beech "curly," I have to shake my head in frustration. Not only are they mistaken (and typically unwilling to listen to a second opinion), but now they are also spreading their nonsense to anyone who will listen.

PROBLEMS WITH SPALTED WOOD

I first learned of the punky quality of spalted wood the hard way. Spalting is a fungal degradation of the wood. Before I had my own lathe, I would go out to my friend Greg's shop, where there was an ancient beast of a lathe that had two speeds governed by a simple pulley arrangement. Of course, there were no markings indicating which was slow and which was fast, and neither of us could remember, so we ended up just guessing. If this was not enough, when I mounted the rectangular blank between centers (it was about four inches square by nine inches long) I did not notice that the tail stock was centered in the middle of a punky section of wood.

Not being complete fools, Greg and I at least had the common sense to stand off to the side (out of the line of fire) when we turned on the lathe. As you can guess, it was in fact set at high speed. The blank started to spin, and then shake, and the next thing we knew and before we could get the lathe turned off, the blank was launched halfway across the room. It actually had a fairly impressive hang time to its flight, and if nothing else came of it, we leaned two very important lessons:
1. Always stand out of the line of fire when turning on any lathe.
2. Never directly mount screws, drive centers, or tail stocks in punky wood.

A jumble of cherry burl.

When using a figured wood for a small turning, I have found that the tighter the figure, the stronger the effect. If you turn an object that is only an inch tall out of a diffusely figured wood, you may not capture enough of the patterning to be as effective as it could. A little figure could end up being visually confusingly and counter-productive to your design.

Burls

If there is anything more enjoyable than turning figured wood, it would have to be turning burls. The chaotic patterning found in most burls will impart an inherently fascinating quality to your work that will almost guarantee success. You would have to try hard to turn an unattractive object out of a burl (although I must say that I have managed to do so). Turning a burl is like cutting a diamond: even if you do mess it up, it is still a diamond. The problem with burls is that because the design of the wood is so strong, it can be difficult to create a turning that will not be overwhelmed by the wood itself.

Spalting

Spalting—a fungal degradation in wood—can occur in many species of wood, but seems to be particularly prevalent with maples. The black lines that course through a spalted sample are the result of a fungus invading the cells of the wood. Spalting can occur to varying degrees, from light to heavy, and can even be promoted by leaving the wood out in a damp environment. If it is left for too long, it will eventually lead to the wood's decay. Often you find "punky" areas in spalted wood that are prone to crumbling rather then clean cutting.

The only caution that you need to have in mind when turning spalted wood is that you will end up releasing the fungus into the air, which has been linked to serious respiratory problems if inhaled.

ALTERNATIVE MATERIALS

While many woodturners will never venture beyond the realm of mounting wood on their lathes, there are several non-wood materials available for your turning enjoyment.

The best source for finding alternative materials is knife-maker suppliers. Custom knife-makers use a wonderful variety of natural materials in the handle of their knives, and almost all of them can be turned on the lathe. If you are looking for kudu horn, hippopotamus teeth, or sambar stag antlers, this is the place to look.

Ivory

Ivory has always been a staple of the specialized "hardwood and ivory" turner. Unfortunately, there are several reasons why ivory is no longer a suitable material for most contemporary turners.

1. Legal ivory is in scarce supply.
2. It is extremely politically incorrect to use (normally I do not bother myself with political correctness, but this time I have to admit that I'm in support of it).
3. Transporting raw and finished ivory turnings across state, provincial, and international borders may be restricted by law (trade in ivory was banned under the CITES Act, although there is a possibility that this may be changing).
4. Even if you can find legal ivory, it will be very expensive.

That said, there are still two types of ivory available on the market today. The first is estate ivory, which is ivory that has been in the country prior to the importation ban. The

A. W. Jones,
Staunton chess patterns,
alternative ivory

(Photo by Tony Boase)

problem with estate ivory is that it is difficult to prove beyond a shadow of a doubt that it is genuine pre-ban ivory and not recently smuggled ivory being represented as estate.

The safe alternative is to use fossil ivory. This ivory comes from mastodon, mammoth, and to a lesser extent walrus, and can easily be distinguished from the modern stuff. The advantages to using fossil ivory is that it is easily distinguishable from new, the animal has already been dead for 30,000 years or so, it can be freely transported across most borders, and some samples may be tinted in a wonderful variety of colors due to the natural minerals in the soil where it has lain. The only limitation with fossil ivory is that it is only available in relatively small pieces—which suits the small-scale turner just fine.

Another alternative to African ivory is the tagua nut. This is a small, whitish nut that can be turned quite effectively and is capable of holding fine detail. The only problem with tagua nuts is that there is an irregular void in the middle of the nut which your must work around.

Bone

Bone is another of the traditional turning materials. It works quite well on the lathe, it is capable of holding extremely fine details, and it polishes to a high luster. The most difficult aspect of turning bone is roughing it out to the round. Take your time and proceed with care. You do not want to be overly aggressive with it because of the brittleness of the material. The round blank responds favorably to either the skew or the scraper. In fact, bone and similar alternative materials are one of the only times that I will consider using a scraper on spindle turning.

While you could process the raw bone yourself, I purchase mine already prepared from the local pet supply store.

Using a skew to scrape bone. It is possible to turn exceptionally fine detail in this material.

(Photo by Peter Stevens)

BENEFITS OF STABILIZED WOOD

1. The process of stabilization renders the wood totally dimensionally stable, which is particularly useful for lidded containers and the like.

2. The stabilization process also solidifies any soft or punky areas in spalted or decayed wood, regardless of the degree of decay, allowing the use of what would otherwise be unworkable.

3. Color can be completely infused, throughout the thickness of the wood.

4. The wood does not need to be finished, and can be buffed to a high gloss, rivaling that of an exotic species.

5. In some cases, it can actually improve the working characteristics of the wood.

Antler

Antler is an interesting material for turning. The use of it is ecologically sound, as antlers are not the same as horns, and are shed on a yearly basis. I have seen antlers from moose, elk, and various species of deer all effectively turned on the lathe. The working properties of the antler are generally good, although there is a porous inner section that needs to be reinforced with cyanoacrylate glue as you turn.

MAN-MADE MATERIALS

I have not used very many of the man-made materials in my turning. It's not that there is nothing of interest, it is just that I am having so much fun turning the natural materials that I simply have not gotten around to it.

STABILIZED WOOD

Stabilized wood is an interesting development that has many advantages for woodturning. Wood is stabilized in a process whereby the natural moisture in the piece of wood is replaced with an inert acrylic-like substance. The process is basically one of reducing the moisture content in the raw wood down to four to six percent, and then in a vacuum injecting the acrylic (and a dye if so desired) until one hundred percent penetration has been achieved.

Stabilized wood is priced by the figure and by the pound. While you can purchase pre-stabilized wood from a supplier, a more economical method is to send a partially turned piece to a processor, who will treat your workpiece and then return it to you to finish your turning.

Kip Christensen, "Lidded Jewelry Bowl," elk antler, ebony, turquoise, 1¾" high by 3⅝" diameter.

(Photos by Photocraft, Orem, UT)

6

Kip Christensen,
"Vase,"
cocobolo, turquoise,
2⅜" high by
1¾" diameter.
(Photo by Photocraft, Orem, UT)

FINISHES AND EMBELLISHMENTS

*To know anything will involve a profound
sensation of ignorance.*

JOHN RUSKIN

 There are only two reasons why we need to apply a finish to a small-scale turning. The first is to protect the object from grimy hands and premature wear, and the second is to try to enhance the final appearance of the new creation.

The finish that is most suited to your turning will ultimately be dependent on the intended function of that particular object. If your turning is intended for use, then you will want to use something that will protect the object and will also be compatible to the role it has been designed for. For example, if you have turned a salt shaker or anything else that will be coming into contact with food, then you will want to use a finish that is totally benign to the user once it has fully cured.

If your object is purely decorative in nature, you will have an unlimited number of finishes or embellishments available for your use. This is assuming, of course, that you even choose to apply one in the first place.

FUNCTIONAL FINISHES

The finish that is applied to a functional turning is ultimately determined by the item's use. It should enhance the object and at the same time protect both turning and person. Not many small-scale turnings are designed to come into direct contact with food. Such use, along with turnings for children (i.e., baby's rattle), defines two of the most demanding responsibilities for proper finishing.

There is a belief circulating among the woodworking community that dictates the commonly acceptable finishes for food-related objects. This belief basically restricts us to the use of the various non-toxic oil finishes (walnut, pure tung, mineral), wax, or

*William R. Duce,
spinning top; ziricote
with boxwood.*

(Photo by Peter Stevens)

shellac. Cooking oils are generally to be avoided (corn, peanut) since they can turn rancid. The main problem with the natural oils is that these "oils" are never truly dry, and require frequent reapplication to retain their original look.

The other "oils" which can be found on the market (Danish, tung, Watco, along with a slew of others) have all had metallic dryers added to them so that they can completely cure into a thin coating. While the non-toxic oils can be ingested in a liquid state (but I would not do it), ingesting the liquid oils that have had the dryers added will likely result in a finish to all of your turning days, if not your life.

Wax provides a basic, if somewhat cursory, finish that is more decora-tive than functional. While it can safely come into contact with food, it, along with the oils, provides little in the way of long-term protection. If you use either of these finishes, you can count on frequent re-appli-cation to maintain the object's origi-nal luster.

Shellac, on the other hand, is an easy-to-use finish which has never really received the mainstream fol-lowing it deserves. Once cured, it is perfectly safe, offers good protec-tion, can be finished to a gloss coat-ing (while the other food-safe coat-ings are generally matte), and is easy to use.

So what makes cured shellac per-fectly safe, whereas in a liquid state it would likely blind if not kill you? The answer lies in the carrier (also referred to as the solvent)—that being the part of any finish that keeps it in a liquid form. In the case of shellac, the carrier is denatured alcohol, a definite "no-no" to ingest. The alcohol in the shellac evaporates as it dries, leaving the natural shellac on your turning. Carriers are an inte-gral part of any finish, and most for-mulated finishes use those that are certainly contrary to longevity if ingested.

In the case of pure, all-natural oils, the oil is a liquid at room tempera-ture and thus does not need a carri-er. This is also the reason that they need to have chemical dryers added to them in order that they cure at room temperature.

William R. Duce, container, big leaf maple, African blackwood, 3¼" by 2", (turned to hold a friends scholastic medal, thus the flat bot-tom in the interior).

(Photo by Peter Stevens)

In the case of water-based finishes, it is not the carrier that you want to avoid, but the binding agent or finish itself. With these, the chemicals that form the film or finish are not to be ingested.

The only voice of dissension in this little debate is the strong argument by respected professional finishers (who are actually nothing more than chemists disguised in flannel) that most finishes are actually quite benign once they have fully cured. After all of the carrier has evaporated, and as long as the integrity of the finish has not been compromised, then it is unlikely that food simply coming into contact with the cured finish will ever make anyone ill. Of course, there are no long-term studies to either confirm or refute this argument, but it seems to be logical to me.

The safest finish to use on anything that you have concerns about is nothing at all. There is no law stating that everything you make out of wood needs to have a barrier slathered upon it before it can be considered complete. Even the verb "finish" is a bit of a misnomer. Perhaps we should instead be calling it "that final step where we slop stuff all over our finely turned objects." The finish on most turnings simply magnifies the grain of the wood, and if you like it as it is, then why not leave well enough alone? If you have ever seen an antique dough bowl that has collected a century's worth

of wear, then it will be obvious that using nothing works quite well, thank you very much.

The other area of concern regarding functional finishes is for those projects that are intended for use by small children. These items, such as baby rattles, toys, and games, all have a good chance of eventually ending up in children's mouths. The simplest route to take is to treat them exactly the same as we did for projects coming into contact with food.

This last area is not really much of a concern of mine due to the size of most of the objects that I create. If there is the potential for a turning to end up in the mouth, then I think the greater threat is swallowing the object rather than ingesting its finish. Whenever dealing with turnings intended for small children, you should always err on the side of caution. Check with local agencies for safety guidelines on children's toys.

But let's face it, the majority of the small-scale turnings that we create will never come into contact with food or into the mouths of babes. It is with these objects, the ones we create for the enjoyment of turning or to exorcize a design that has been floating around in our craniums, that we can truly let our imaginations roam.

For a straight-ahead finish—simply intended as a clear coat to enhance the grain of the wood—my finishes of choice are shellac, wax, or one of the oils.

Applying a turner's polish to the figured maple candleholder.

SHELLAC

Finishing a ring box. I am using wax applied with a fine Scotch-Brite pad. Boxwood requires little in the way of a finish.

If there was ever a perfect all-around finish, shellac would be it. This adaptable little excrement of the lac bug excels at almost anything we could ask of it. You can purchase shellac in flake or a dissolved form, but because the shelf life of dissolved shellac is only a year or so, I prefer to buy it in flake form to mix myself.

The more that shellac is refined, the lighter the color of the flakes. It can range from raw to blond, with several grades in between. I like to use the orange grade of shellac; I find it imparts a nice warm tone to maple and other light-colored woods.

While shellac is my finish of choice for higher-end gallery turn-ings, for production work I will usually use one of the popular turner's polishes that are commonly available. These finishes are actually a form of pre-mixed shellac and oil that are almost foolproof to apply, dry quickly, and provide a nice gloss to the finished object. If I am working on a run of bobbins, the speed and quality of the turner's polish is impossible to beat.

The application of this type of polish is quite simple. With the lathe turned off, apply a generous but not sloppy amount of polish to your turning, wait a few seconds, and then turn on the lathe and buff with a clean rag. With lace bobbins, I do not even bother to turn off the lathe; I just make a couple of passes with a saturated rag along the turning bobbin, wait for a count of "one

APPLYING FINISH

To apply finish, I use a method which I modified slightly from an article featuring Michael Mode, in *Woodshop News*. (See Michael Mode's work in the Gallery section.)

The first step is to make sure that your turning is free of any blemishes or sanding marks. I will usually take it at least up to 320 grit, but usually 600 for fine-grained wood. While manually revolving the turning, seal the wood with a bit of thin cyano-acrylate glue on a cotton pad taped to a cotton swab. After this dries, in a minute or two, prepare a strip of cotton cloth about one by three inch-es. To this you will apply the dissolved shellac on one end and mineral oil on the other. Turn the lathe on a low speed, and taking particular care with any voids or sharp edges, start at one end of your turning and slowly lead with the shellac end of the cloth, so that the oil-impregnated end will follow immediately. Make three or four pass-es like this, and then turn the lathe off and let the turning cure. If you like, you can apply multiple coats this way, waiting overnight before the next application.

The most applications I have ever used was seven or eight, to the cocobolo handle of an awl. This created a deep-gloss finish that accentu-ated the natural proper-ties of the cocobolo and has never failed to elicit a favorable response from anyone who has seen it.

SEARCHING FOR THE ULTIMATE FINISH

My search for the ultimate finish led me to Mark Tinsky, at the American Smoking Company. Mark has been handcrafting custom pipes for the past eighteen years, and is one of the leaders in his field. I contacted Mark because what other small wooden object is subjected to the same stress as a pipe? Pipes have a fire ignited in a bowl, only to have it fanned by oxygen sucked through a spindle, which if the smoker is not careful, will be mixed with the saliva from his mouth.

I do not know about you, but this certainly beats anything I have ever put a turning through! The wood that Mark uses to create all of his pipes is prime Grecian Plateaux briar, a tight-grained root-burl. As a finish, Mark will sand until there are no marks or blemishes remaining, and then buff with jeweler's rouge on a cotton wheel, followed by carnuba wax on a flannel wheel. Simple enough, and yet it provides a deep, rich finish that is easy to touch up if need be. There are other concoctions of wax, shellac, or lacquer that other pipemakers may use, but the results of Mark's method speak for themselves.

---

blackwood, two blackwood," and then buff it off with a clean rag. Easy as can be.

I rarely use an oil finish. The only time I do is when I have extensively carved the object and would have problems using one of the other methods. In this instance, oil easily reaches into all of the little nooks and crannies and does an admirable job.

Patience is the key when using an oil. Thoroughly apply it, wait however long the container says, and then wipe it off. Leave it overnight, and repeat as many times as are necessary. This type of finish is about one of the simplest and it is favored by many turners. Still, I find that it takes too long to reach the sheen I prefer. The one caveat with oil, which cannot be repeated often enough, is to dispose of all of your rags in a proper manner. I keep any rag that has come into contact with oil in a jar filled with water until I can properly dispose of it.

The final step that I take in finishing is to apply a wax top coat. While wax is not normally a very protective finish on its own, it does make an excellent complement to a primary finish.

You can apply the wax in a variety of ways. The easiest is to apply by hand a thin coating of furniture wax with a clean white cotton rag, wait a minute or two for it dry, and then buff it off. The next step up the ladder is to apply the same wax to the spinning, turning with a fine grade of Scotch Brite pad (I use the white). Wait a couple of minutes, and then buff off. This is often more than enough for blackwood and other exotics.

This is simply a small neoclassical shaped urn that functions well as a toothpick holder. The grain of the apple wood runs along the length of the piece. This is the time to apply your finish of choice.

7

William R. Duce, striped ebony commemorative baby rattle, with three enclosed rings, 4¾" by 1⅜".

(Photo by Peter Stevens)

This is strictly intended to be a presentation piece for the proud parents; the rings are too small and possibly delicate to survive a baby's mauling, and the ball is also undersized and could possibly prove to be a choking hazard (why take the risk?).

SAFETY

Whoever undertakes to hew wood for the master carpenter rarely escapes injuring his own hand.

LAO-TZU

*Michael Lee,
"Storm Pattern
Starfish," cocobolo,
5½" diameter
by 3⅓" high.*

(Photo by Hugo de Vries)

 Turning small-scale objects is by far one of the safest of all woodworking practices. While mishaps do occasionally occur, they are not usually very serious and are much less likely to end up with your taking a trip to the local emergency room.

I can state positively that in all of my years of turning small objects, I have never had an accident befall me. There have been plenty of mishaps, but never an accident. The difference between the two is that if you were to repeat all the steps that led up to your incident, and the results were exactly the same, then obviously there was nothing accidental about it. Just because you did not realize at the time that what you were doing could have unsatisfactory results does not make it an accident.

The only ways that we can protect ourselves when turning is to be aware of what we are doing at all times and to know what the possible results of our actions may be. If you do not know what is going to happen when you stick a scraper into a natural-edged blank spinning at 1000 rpm, then perhaps you should think twice before doing so. If something does not feel right, then it probably isn't. On a good day, when I get that nagging feeling, I will back off and reexamine what I am doing until I become comfortable with my actions. On a bad day, I will press ahead and, more times than not, totally muddle up what I am working on. The only times when I have ever even moderately injured my person while turning (I class a moderate injury as one that results in a string of cuss words and a bandage) is when, through my own inattentiveness, I have brushed my hand against a spinning chuck or belt. Skin gets shed, but it is always my fault due to a lapse of concentration.

BE AWARE OF WHAT YOU ARE DOING

You should devlop your own approach to working on the lathe. Develop a written or mental checklist that you follow each time you get ready to turn. Comments on safety are included in almost every chapter; here I'll remind you of the things I suggest you consider.

Once you are organized, able to concentrate, and have secured any needed protective devices, you are ready to work. The first step is to rough-turn the blank.

Your Working Environment

Before you start, keep in mind that nothing is as important as a comfortable and efficient work environment to ensure that your turning experiences are both enjoyable and safe. Make sure to keep your work area neat and clean. As you should be aware, excess dust can become a breathing hazard. Regularly evaluate your workspace for ergonomic efficiency—is it comfortable to work in?—and for lighting conditions. Good lighting is essential for the safe use of sharp tools and a high-speed lathe or any power tool.

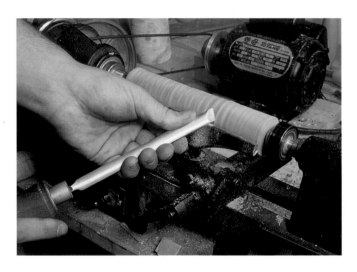

As you set up your work, make sure that you are familiar with your equipment. If it is new to you, consult the owner's manual, especially to see if there are adjustments or safety-related devices of which you should be aware. Be sure the switch operates properly. Never allow someone else to turn on the power for you, and never leave any machine unattended with the power on. Keep children well supervised.

Are You Ready to Work?

Your basic safety checklist should include an assessment of your mental and physical acuity.

Are you able to concentrate and work safely? Never work when you are tired or taking medication. Take a break when you become tired. Don't rush the job, and avoid distractions such as talking with someone while working.

Your safety checklist should also include making sure that you are wearing appropriate clothing and necessary protective gear. Your clothing should be comfortable but not loose. You should remove all jewelry and tie back long hair. Wear protective glasses, goggles, and/or a face shield. You might also find your work more comfortable if you have earplugs or muffs.

Safety with Your Lathe

Be familiar with your lathe; know all of the parts and how they operate. Before you switch on, make sure the workpiece is well mounted and secure. Turn the workpiece over by hand and make sure that it clears the tool rest. Once you begin to work, stop or slow down the machine before you check your progress with a template or caliper. Move the tool rest well out of the way before sanding. When you are polishing with a cloth, never roll the cloth around your fingers, but rather make a pad, in case the cloth gets caught by the spinning work or drive center.

William R. Duce,
free-form big leaf maple
burl and rosewood,
3¼" by 3⅜";
big leaf maple burl
and rosewood,
3⅞" by 2⅛";
poplar burl,
3⅝" by 2½".

(Photo by Peter Stevens)

Part of your normal safe working practice should include moving the tool rest out of the way before sanding—as here with the final sanding of the ring box project.

Usually on those rare occasions when a blank comes out of the chuck, it simply rolls around harmlessly on the lathe bed—damaging the wood more than anything else. The only exception I've had is once when I had a bone bobbin self-destruct. I had attempted to take "just one more pass" on the neck of the bobbin. It was not until three days later that I finally found the head of the bobbin. It had splintered off, leaving a sharp fragment that could have easily resulted in a serious injury to the eye.

From this experience, I suspect that other brittle materials will behave in an identical manner. While I am admittedly negligent at times about wearing a face shield, I always make it a hard-and-fast rule to wear eye protection—protective glasses or goggles—whenever turning.

I emphasize again that the most serious threat to your safety when turning small objects is wood dust. The steps that can be taken to control this invisible hazard can be found in Chapter 4, "Your Working Environment."

8

*William R. Duce,
"Vessel,"
cherry burl,
2¼" high
by 3¾" diameter.*

(Photo by Peter Stevens)

TAKING THE PLUNGE

No bird soars too high, if he soars with his own wings.
WILLIAM BLAKE

Craig Lossing,
Maple, ebony, plywood,
6" high by 9" wide.

(Photo by Craig Lossing)

 We all bring our own perspective to the fine art of small-scale turning. This has resulted in a wonderful diversity of turnings, and yet there is a unifying influence common to all small-scale work—the "economy of scale" that has been used in its creation.

ECONOMY OF SCALE

What I mean when I refer to economy of scale is the influence that the object transmits to the individual viewing the work, as well as to the artisan who is creating it.

When we examine any small-scale turning, our focus is quickly brought down to the object's perspective. If we wish to receive its full impact, we will be forced to get up close and personal with it. Unlike larger turnings, small-scale work cannot be effectively viewed from several feet away. Ideally, we will touch the object and nestle it in our hand.

Immediately upon doing so, we have doubled our sensory input of the piece, which can only magnify our reaction to the object. Feel the object's weight in your hand—does it inspire confidence or apprehension? Turn it over, look inside. Take advantage of its dimension by viewing it from all angles and perspectives—something that would be impossible with some larger works.

Handling small-scale pieces, it quickly becomes apparent that they are intimate objects, there for the viewer and the viewer alone. When you are focused on a diminutive turning, all the other objects surrounding it will temporarily cease to exist. A type of tunnel vision will anchor your gaze to this one, individual piece. This is the response that such objects should generate. They will take us down to their scale, rather than our trying to fit them to the environment around us.

Our focus is quickly brought down to the object's perspective, as we compare the completed turning, a chessman, to the original template.

From the turner's perspective, an economy of scale will offer all the aforementioned features, along with a few additional perks. The first and most obvious is that turning small pieces requires far less in materials (and debatably, tools) than turning larger objects. And for turning, which can be an admittedly wasteful process in terms of volume of wood in the final product versus volume of shavings on the floor, using smaller pieces means less of a monetary and environmental cost. Additionally, the small-scale turner will be able to utilize materials that are simply not available in a larger size. Do you want to turn a box out of a hippopotamus tooth? Not a problem. Or how about inlaying a piece of black-lip mother-of-pearl into the lid? Again, not a problem.

To create small-scale turnings you need neither a full-time shop nor a lot of space to dedicate to your pursuit. In fact, all of the objects I have made in this book were done in a one-bedroom high-rise apartment. By using a little common sense (and that's about all I can spare), you will be able to get along quite well in a restricted environment.

William R. Duce, twisted candleholder; African blackwood, 2¾" by 5½".

(Photo by Peter Stevens)

DESIGN

Designing a turning should be an exciting and liberating experience. You should have fun with it. Do what you want, and do not feel constrained by any pre-set notions or expectations. For the small-scale object, your only limitation is that you are creating a uniquely personal object as opposed to a communal popcorn or salad bowl.

Identifying the purpose of your creation is always the first step to any effective design. If it is a functional piece, then your design will have certain parameters which it must meet to ensure its usability. After these are realized, you can then embellish the object to your heart's content. For example, a lace bobbin must have an area in which to store thread, as well as a head design that will allow the thread to be easily knotted on. Beyond this, the design of a bobbin is totally up to your individual whims and fancies.

If your turning is intended as a decorative object, then the door is wide open for you to do whatever you like. While it may seem that these would be easier pieces to design, they are in fact more difficult since you do not have any sort of guidelines suggesting where you should start or stop. When an object's function is easily recognizable, such as with a lace bobbin, chessman, bowl, or whatever, the designer and viewer will have something to compare it with in order to judge whether or not it is a success. If it does not have a comparable equal, then many people will be at a loss to consider it strictly on the basis of its own merit. How many times have you heard, "That's nice, what is it?"

For the novice turner, all that one can say is: Keep your eyes open, and eventually you will find your way. Examining the work of other turners will show what is possible, but not necessarily what you should be doing. Our ultimate goal is to develop our own distinct visual identity.

William R. Duce, bowls; Russian olive, 4⅜" by 1¾"; English elm burl, 3⅝" by ⅞".

(Photo by Peter Stevens)

INSPIRATION

Inspiration is such a vast and personal experience that it is a little difficult to talk about in general terms. We all live in an incredibly rich and diverse world where, at every turn, we are constantly bombarded by visual information and stimuli. As developing designers, it is our job to assimilate as much of this as we can, and adapt it to our own personal visions. The mantra of the designer should be to look at everything and miss nothing.

SKETCHING

I believe that a sketch book should be an integral part to any turner's tool kit. The purpose of a sketch book is not to show how well we can or cannot draw, but to be a visual diary for recording any interesting ideas we may have. Like any diary, it is a personal journal that is not intended for a public viewing. Knowing that no one else will ever see it should help to liberate the hand and allow the pen to roam freely across the pages.

David Sengel, "Hummingbird," 6" by 7", cherry, rose, locust, trifoliate orange thorns, black lacquer, India ink.

(Photo by Michael Siede)

The base is laurel root and the flowers are filbert husks. The bird is turned on 11 centers, carved to finish, and is hollow with a lid in its back.

There are two types of sketch books that I prefer. The first is a plain hardbound version available at any art supply store. The second is a simple notebook that is one-inch graph paper rather than blank pages. I use the blank book to explore basic shapes and form. The graph paper notebook comes in handy when I am trying to refine the size and proportions of various turnings, such as when I'm designing chess men.

The act of sketching is a little chaotic and rarely predictable. Free your hand on the page, and let it go where it will. You may only end up with a page full of doodles, but since you are training your eye along with your hand, you just may find something of interest in that page. Details are my last concern when sketching. While they may add greatly to my

turning, if the overall proportions are wrong, no amount of details will ever be able to correct it.

ORIGINALITY

They say that imitation may be the greatest form of flattery. While this may be true in many instances, it certainly does not apply if you are passing off your imitation as an original piece for a show or exhibition. If you are a studio turner, then exhibiting a work that you have copied perhaps a bit too closely is a quick form of professional suicide (which is why you will rarely if ever see it done by this group). If you are an enthusiastic hobbyist, then there is absolutely nothing wrong with reproducing the work of another turner, so long as it is for your own enjoyment.

Imitating another person's work has been the traditional method of learning for both artists and craftsmen. The reason, in part, was that everyone being trained should be able to carry on the work in the same style as his or her master. Today, however, it is more important for artisans to develop their own style, and copying another's is generally a means of learning new techniques and methods. While most turners will not object to your copying their work, presenting it as your own is a definite mistake. The reason (other than possible legal and ethical considerations) is that the styles of famous turners are all well known. While their work may not be trade-

GOLDEN RULES OF WOODTURNING

1. Turning should always be fun.

2. Turning is a personal exploration, so satisfy your inner muse first.

3. A successful turning is an equal balance between technique and design.

4. The success of your project is dependent upon a positive attitude, not expensive tools or secret tricks.

5. There is no shame in making a mistake; just try not to make the same one twice.

6. Never stop looking for inspiration, especially outside the world of turning.

7. A finished turning will always look better than one only half turned. By finishing what you start you just may surprise yourself.

8. The proper way to use any tool is whichever way works best for you.

9. Never be discouraged by people saying, "That's pretty, what is it?"

10. Design gimmicks and fads have the approximate life span of free burl at a turner's convention. Avoid them at all costs.

marked in the legal sense, it certainly is in the visual. If you presented a scoop for sale in a style that Richard Raffan has been making for twenty years, not only will it look bad on you, but it will also place the remainder of your work in doubt.

The problem (which can be experienced) is, say, that you have arrived at a design—apparently all on your own—only to find that someone else has been producing a similar object for a number of years. The solution is not so simple. In some cases, the form may be so general that it cannot be attributed to any one individual. In other cases, however, the individual who first presented the work will always be considered the designer, and all others mere copiers.

Needle cases, left to right, African blackwood, 1" by 3"; ebony and big leaf maple, ⅞" by 3¾"; African Blackwood, ¾" by 3¾".

(Photo by Peter Stevens)

PROJECTS

In selecting the featured small-scale turning projects, I have tried to choose those which will be of interest to both the beginner and the experienced turner. None of these projects is exceptionally challenging—they are intended to be used only as a launching pad for your own development as both a turner and designer. The most important requirement for their successful completion is a basic confidence in your own skills. Once you have achieved this, you will be capable of tackling any project regardless of how complicated it may initially appear.

My intention is to present these projects, as with the earlier chapters, from the perspective of the serious artisan, that is, someone who creates these small objects out of choice rather than as a means of simply using up his off-cuts. You will discover, perhaps, that bigger is not in fact better and that a finely turned small-scale object is the equal, if not the champion, of its "big-boned cousins."

Most of the techniques of turning are actually quite basic—all that is required to master them is time, patience, and practice. My premise is not so much to offer a "how to" as it is to explain "why to."

TOOL HANDLES

I believe that every tool should come from the factory without a handle.

While factory handles are generally quite serviceable, there is no reason why we, as turners, should not turn our own handles to meet our individual methods and our own hands.

Tool handles; figured walnut awl, figured maple skew.

(Photo by Peter Stevens)

The other reason that I prefer making my own handles is that it is an easy way to improve the aesthetics of the tool. I have been known to collect a few antique tools now and again, and the variety of handles that you find on antique turning tools will usually exceed those offered by most contemporary manufacturers. While improving the aesthetics of the handle may not necessarily improve our turning, it will increase our fondness for the tool.

The handle I turned for this project is based on the typical nineteenth-century English standard. I've added a few beads, but the general shape is the same. The wood is soft curly maple, part of a group of two-by-fours that I purchased from a mill that was going to use them to make shipping palettes.

Traditionally when you attach the ferrule, you would use a punch to keep it in place, but I apply a dab of epoxy instead.

1. Rough-turn the blank to 1½" by 7½".

2. With the calipers set to the inside dimension of the ferrule, turn the tenon to size with a parting tool. Then attach the ferrule.

3. Rough-shape the handle with a gouge.

4. Use the Bill Jones point tool to cut any beads and generally refine the overall shape.

5. With the handle sanded and finished, drill the hole to fit the tool.

CRIBBAGE COUNTERS

Cribbage counters; all of African blackwood; carved with bone; with a garnet cabochon set in a sterling bezel; bone with a garnet cabochon set in a sterling bezel, largest dimensions ¼" by 1¾".

(Photo by Peter Stevens)

Some of my earliest memories are centered around Sunday-afternoon card games at my grandparents'. I was probably only about four years old at the time, and I had to lay all of my cards out along the table because my hands were too small to hold them (this was for rumole). I can remember getting really annoyed with anyone whenever they would take a peek at them.

From these humble beginnings I went on to learn most of the traditional card games, but cribbage was always one of our favorites. And our favorite variation of the game was one we called "cutthroat." The only difference between this and the regular game was that you could count any points that your opponent missed. Normally, this would not happen very often, but when you throw in a libation and try to have the other player purposefully miss scoring, things can certainly get interesting.

.The typical store-bought cribbage counters are ugly plastic extrusions that have no place in an artisan's home. Creating your own counters is really quite easy.

The first step is to determine the size of the holes in your board and how far apart they are spaced. You have to make sure that the diameter of your counters is slightly smaller than the distance between holes, so that two will fit side by side. Other than this, the design is totally open to your imagination.

When I turn counters, I like to use close-grained exotic off-cuts, bone, and similar material. I will often leave a small tenon on the top to fit a sterling-silver band inset with a semi-precious cabochon.

1. Use a Jacobs chuck to hold the blank, and then rough out the blackwood with a ¼" skew.

2, 3. Shape the profile of the counter using the skew with the point . . .

4, 5. . . . both leading and trailing.

6. Cut a cove with a ⅛"
miniature gouge.

7. Check the taper with a vernier caliper to ensure that it will fit in a ⅛" hole.

8. Sand with a Scotch-Brite pad.

9. Apply a furniture-grade wax on a Scotch-Brite pad.

10. Part it off with the tip of a skew.

LACE BOBBINS

Turning lace bobbins is the perfect project to help you master the art of spindle turning. The first bobbins that I made were absolute monstrosities, as I did not know any lace makers and had only seen them in magazines. After finally figuring out the proper dimensions, I went on to have great fun making them out of all sorts of wood and bone.

Bobbins are one of those objects that can be as simple or as complex as you want to make them. The midland style of bobbin, which is illustrated here, is open to all manner of variations.

The greatest difficulty you will encounter when turning a bobbin will be preventing the bobbin from "whipping" when you are turning the neck. My rule of thumb for turning the neck is to work it as thin as I possibly can. Turning a thinner or longer neck will allow the lace maker to store more thread, but will also increase the chances of the bobbin's breaking on the lathe.

I used a piece of ⅜" square by 4¾" long bocote for this project. When selecting a blank, search for something that is straight and finely grained.

Midland style bobbins; ebony, prima vera, African blackwood, prima vera, ebony, prima vera, tulipwood, and bone, ⁵⁄₁₆" by 4¾".

(Photo by Peter Stevens)

While you can purchase a drive center made especially for turning bobbins, I made my own out of a piece of boxwood. The easiest way to make one is to record the length, width at the base, and width at the top of the drive center that came with your lathe (likely a four-prong drive), and then turn a piece of boxwood to match these dimensions (this is of course assuming that your lathe has a Morse taper to begin with). Once you have it close, try fitting it into the taper until it seats all the way and revolves without any vibration when the lathe is turned on. Next, drill a ⅜" hole in the face of the boxwood, and then square it up with a small chisel and turn whatever design you like onto the side.

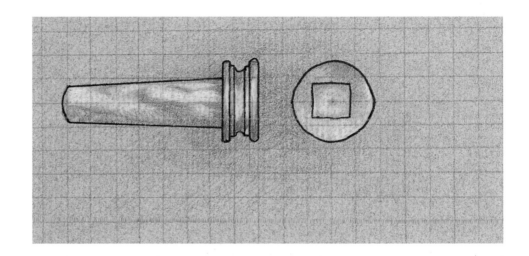

(Drawing is full size, on a quarter-inch grid.) Shop-made bobbin drive.

1. I am inserting a boxwood drive chuck which I made to fit the No. 1 Morse taper of my lathe.

2. Make a stop cut at the head of the bobbin. This is to prevent the wood from splintering out along its length once you start to rough it out with the skew.

3. Rough out the blank with the leading point of the skew. You could also use a gouge, but I find the skew quicker.

4. Establish the layout and proportions of the bobbin, and then shape the head.

5. Use the ⅛" gouge to cut a cove in the base.

6. Finish shaping the head.

7, 8. Cutting the neck down to size with the skew (this one was thicker than normal at ⁵/₃₂"). This is actually the second bobbin that I turned for this project. The first broke at this point due to the grain running out of the blank. Use your finger to support the bobbin from the other side once it starts to whip.

9. Applying two coats of a turner's polish. Bobbins need to have an inert finish so the lace will not pick up any color from either the wood or the finish. All that is left is to part it off, and drill a hole in the base for a spangle.

NEEDLE CASES

Needle cases were one of the first production items I made on the lathe. They are a challenging but fun project, and sure to be a hit with anyone who sews.

You can use almost any wood for this project, and I will often purchase packages of ¾" pen blanks to use. Needle cases also lend themselves to all manner of decoration and carving; the options are endless.

Needle cases; chechen, ebony with big leaf maple burl, and figured maple.

(Photo by Peter Stevens)

1. After turning the blank until it is round, part the wood into two pieces. I find that separating it into thirds works well for most of my designs.

2. With the top of the case held in your chuck, drill a 7/16" hole 5/16" deep for the tenon, then a 5/16" hole 1" deep for the needles. By drilling the hole to this depth, the user will be able to tip the needles into it and select the one they desire.

3. With the base held in the chuck, and the tail stock brought up for support, turn the tenon to just a hair more than 7/16" size, checking with calipers as you go.

4. Continue to cut the tenon to size, frequently stopping the lathe to check the fit.

Different woods will have different tolerances, so this step has to be taken with care.

If you turn the tenon too small, you can try to use cyano-

acrylate to build it back up. I have never been satisfied with the results, however. All that I do is part it off or start all over again.

5. With the tenon fitting nicely, advance the tail stock with a ⁵⁄₁₆" brad point drill bit in the Jacob's chuck until the point of the bit is centered on the tenon. Manually revolve the hand wheel while advancing the tail stock, until you have established that it is in fact centered.

6. Turn the lathe on and drill out the base approximately 1½" to 2" deep.

7. Reassemble both portions on the tail stock, and true up the blank.

8. I will usually turn a few beads where the two halves meet to hide the joint. I always try to create an invisible joint so that it is always a bit of a surprise for whoever opens it the first time.

9. I usually add a couple of coves near the end to supply an area for the user to get a good grip. This is especially important if you has arthritis or other problems with your hands.

10. Do any final shaping or touching up.

11. Touch it up with a little sanding. It should not require much, typically 220 grit or better.

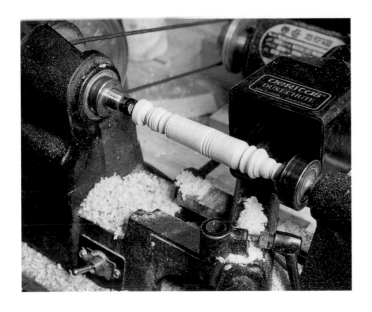

12. A quick swipe with the wax, and a buff, and all that remains to be done is to part it off and touch up the ends.

COASTERS

Coasters; back two are figured maple, front is zebrano.

(Photo by Peter Stevens)

Coasters are a great project and, if you are like me, you will receive satisfaction from creating something that will be used on a regular basis. The design of a coaster can be as simple or as complex as you wish to make it. The only basic requirement is that it can effectively act as a barrier between a cup and the surface it is resting upon.

The stock that I use for most of the coasters that I make is between ¾" and 1" thick, and approximately 4¼" square. For the width, the important measurement is for the flat inside surface that the cup will be set upon. Most mugs are about 3" to 3¼" in diameter, so you will want to allow for a design that will comfortably hold them.

Any wood works well for a coaster. Shorts and off-cuts from the lumberyard work wonderfully. I will typically keep my eye open for any interesting pieces with a nice grain figure or color to them. Remember, they are made to be used every day, so go that extra distance and use something that will distinguish them from the ordinary.

One consideration you may want to incorporate when making your own is to line the bottom with a thin cork to act as a barrier between your cup and the wood. Liquid will be spilled, or cold drinks will perspire, and you will find that the coaster may end up sticking to the bottom of the cup when you pick it up. Personally, this does not bother me, and I have never resorted to using cork. Besides, the cork would obscure any grain pattern of the wood.

The stock for this one is 4¾" by 1" hard curly maple (it came from the same board as the needle case).

1. You can initially mount the blank on whatever chuck you prefer, be it the basic four-screw model that comes with most lathes, glued to a waste block or double-sided tape.

My preferred method is to use a screw chuck. The one I am using here is from Big Tree Tools, Inc., and is basically a production model of what turners have been making for themselves for years.

The chuck consists of a threaded outer body that fits onto your lathe's spindle and then has a replaceable center screw that is held in place with an Allen screw. I replaced the brass screw that came with the chuck with a steel one (actually, I twisted it off in a piece of blackwood).

You can also see that I am using a ¼" plywood spacer between the chuck and blank. This is optional depending upon the length of screw that you have set in the chuck.

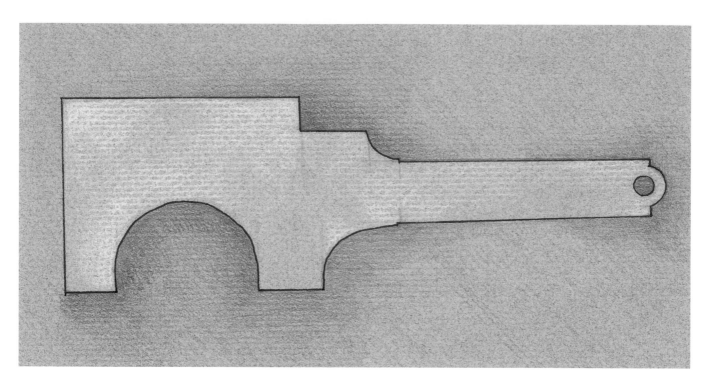

(Drawing is full size.) Everyone who uses a scroll chuck should make themselves one of these simple "go/no go" gauges. Take a piece of thin brass, mark the maximum expansion of the inside jaws on one side and the minimum contraction of the outside jaws on the other, and then cut out your measurements with either a hack or a jeweler's saw.

2. Rough-shape the underside of the coaster with a ⅜" gouge.

3. I like to refine the bottom with a series of beads in order to add some interest to the form.

4. Sheer-cutting the beads with a point tool works surprisingly well.

5. Check the size of the recess with a homemade gauge to see if it will fit into the expansion jaws of your chuck.

6. Once the back has been sanded and a finish applied, the blank can then be remounted in a scroll chuck, and shaping of the interior can begin.

7. Refine the interior form by sheer-scraping. Here I am using a miniature roundnose scraper set in a Stabilax.

When I first saw the Stabilax skew and scraper holder, I thought it was yet another of those gimmicky tools that was only intended to part you from your money rather than part wood from your turnings. But being the open-minded and adventurous guy that I am, I attached it to my ¼" roundnose scraper and gave it a try.

Well, my first impression was wrong. Not only will this tool allow you to sheer-scrape with confidence; more important, it provides some much needed reinforcement to this small scraper. Before I applied the Stabilax, the scraper would flex and chatter, and I rarely used it. After applying the Stablilax, it became as steady as a rock.

8. Sand in the interior surfaces. I have wrapped the tips of my sanding fingers with a high-friction guard tape to avoid burning them when sanding. This tape is designed to stick only to itself, and can be molded and pulled off your fingers and reused between sandings.

9. Apply your finish. In this case, I am using a turner's polish.

Bottom view of a curly birch coaster, featuring an ebonized cherry rope carving, 4⅜" by ⅞".

(Photo by Peter Stevens)

SPINNING TOPS

Spinning tops; briar burl with tulipwood, and ziricote with boxwood.

(Photo by Peter Stevens)

Spinning tops appeal to the child in all of us. Like all of the projects in this book, they can be made as simple or as complicated as you like.

Most tops are made out of a single piece of wood—a great way of doing them if you are using a domestic species. But since I chose to use an exotic, I did not want to waste a lot of the wood that would have been the result of turning a ⅜" spindle out of a 2" piece of timber.

For the design of a top, try to maintain a low center of gravity. Other than that, just have fun.

I am using a 2" round by 1¾" long piece of ziricote, with a boxwood spindle ⅜" by 2½" long.

1. With the ziricote rough-turned and mounted in your chuck, drill a ¼" hole to receive the tenon on the boxwood spindle.

2. True up the top surface, and cut a few beads where the spindle will be entering the top.

3. Turn the rest of the top surface, adding whatever ornamentation you like.

4. Sand the top surface before starting to form the sides.

5. Make a stop cut in front of the chuck with the point tool.

6. Remove the bulk of the sides with a gouge.

7. Refine the sides with the point tool.

8. Part the top off with the leading edge of a skew. This takes a bit of caution, but is not difficult to do. Slowly nibble away at the point, while supporting the body of the top with your hand; . . .

9. . . . eventually, it will come free. I did not have to sand the sides of the top, thanks to the quality of the timber. All I did was lightly buff it with a rotary tool.

10. Turn the boxwood spindle to attach to the top.

11. Attach the two with cyanoacrylate, making sure that the spindle is perfectly perpendicular to the top surface of the top. If you are not right on, then your top will be offbalance.

One way to assist in the alignment is to increase the length of the hole that is drilled to ¾" and the tenon to match. You could also attach the spindle at Step 7, using the tail stock to align it into place and support it for turning.

BOWLS

William R. Duce, bowls; Russian olive, English elm burl, zebrano.

(Photo by Peter Stevens)

Bowls are the mainstay of faceplate turning. For the small-scale turner, most bowls will end up more decorative than functional (although they do work well for people on a reduced-calorie diet). Turning a bowl is really no more difficult than turning a coaster. After all, a coaster is nothing more than a thin bowl.

The possibilities that bowl turning presents are unlimited, and give us the opportunity to really let our creative juices express themselves.

For this project I am working with a piece of 2"-thick-by-4"-round zebrano.

1. With the rough blank mounted on a screw chuck and the tail stock brought up for support, rough-turn the exterior shape.

2. Sheer-scrape the exterior (I am using the point tool) once it has been rough-shaped and the tail stock moved out of the way, so that a dovetailed tenon can be turned to fit into the scroll chuck.

3. Finish the exterior before remounting it to turn the interior.

4. Insert the dove-tailed tenon into the jaws of the chuck.

5. Hog out the interior of the bowl. You can turn the walls to any size you prefer, although the trend these days is towards thinner walls.

6. Sand the interior. When sanding any bowl or spindle, you should always keep your fingers and sandpaper in the lower quadrant, closest to you.

7. This way, the natural revolving action of the lathe will pull the paper. If you sanded in any other position, it would be pushing— which could result in a nasty little injury to your fingers.

8. The finished bowl.

TOOTHPICK HOLDERS

William R. Duce,
toothpick holders;
apple, ziricote.

(Photo by Peter Stevens)

This project does not necessarily have to be a toothpick holder; it is simply a small, neoclassically shaped urn that happens to fulfill this role quite well.

The first thing you will notice when turning this project is that the grain of wood runs along the length of the piece. Hollowing end grain can be more difficult than typical faceplate work where the grains runs across the axis, but it is certainly not beyond any turner's skill.

The wood that I am using is a piece of 2½" long by 1¼" wide apple. It does not have much in the way of grain or figure to it but, like most fruit woods, it turns well and is capable of holding fine detail.

1. With the blank held in the chuck, start by forming the top half of the urn.

2. Continue profiling the bell shape until it forms a gradual curve that terminates at the top of the turnip-shaped bottom.

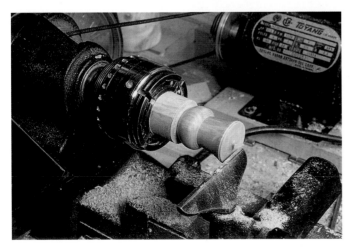

3. With the top portion of the exterior sanded, remove the tail stock and prepare to hollow the urn.

4. Using a ¼" gouge, drill out the top and then gradually turn the walls to a consistent thickness. . . .

5. . . . At this point, you have to decide if you are going to work towards a continuous thickness for all of the top, or leave the turnip portion solid to add mass and increase its stability.

6. Oops! When I was hollowing the sides, I took a little too much from one section so that it became translucent when lighted from behind. I managed to decrease the rest of it so that it would all match, but then when I went to "kiss" it with a light

sanding (and I should have known better), it immediately cracked due to the heat generated by the friction of the sandpaper.

7. Start shaping the base after the top has been shaped and hollowed.

8. With a ⅛" gouge, add a few coves or beads to the base for interest.

9. Do any final sanding, and then apply your finish of choice.

CANDLEHOLDERS

William R. Duce, candleholders; box elder, 3½" by 2¼"; and figured maple, 3¾" by 1¼".

(Photo by Peter Stevens)

Candleholders have always been a staple of the turner's craft. They can range from a nice piece of wood with a hole drilled in it to a finely turned spindle with lots of minute details (as can be seen on the opposite page).

The primary importance of the stand that you make, regardless of its form, is that it be absolutely stable. Even though most of the stands made will never actually hold a lighted candle, we have to design and produce them with the assumption that they will.

You can design your stands following the squat stands that I turn in the project photos or elaborate on your design such as the ziricote stand on the left, or the African blackwood stand on the right that is turned upside down to show the finished base.

This project has been designed to produce relatively simple-looking, somewhat squat stands. Each is made out of a piece of 1" by 4" hard-figured maple. If you wish to increase the height of the stands, then you can either use thicker stock or else turn a cup to fit into the base.

William R. Duce, "Twisted Stand" candleholders; ziricote; African blackwood, 6" high by 3" diameter.

(Photo by Peter Stevens)

1. With the blank mounted in a screw chuck, sheer-cut a profile along the edge of the object. You will be cutting the end grain on the hard maple, so make sure that your tools are absolutely sharp.

2. Turn a shallow catch-basin for any wax with a gouge, followed by a sheer scraper.

3. Establishing the details of the profile with a ⅛" gouge. These gouges can be a little delicate, so you have to be careful not to overextend them when turning large pieces.

4. Turn the recess for the candle. You can add a brass ring to it if you wish, or perhaps one made out of a contrasting wood.

5. The final sanding.

6. Applying a turner's polish.

7. The finished stand, ready for the candle.

RING BOXES

*William R. Duce,
ring boxes; briar burl,
African blackwood,
boxwood.*

(Photo by Peter Stevens)

Ring boxes, and any small box for that matter, are a great deal of fun to create. I like to use them as a replacement for those felt-covered monstrosities supplied by most jewelers. While I can show you how to turn one, it will be up to you to fill it.

I thought it only appropriate to make this box out of box-wood. Not only because of the play on words, but because it turns like a dream.

The dimensions of the piece are 1¼" long by 1½" round.

1. Mount the round blank into a scroll chuck. I do not turn a dovetail for boxes this small in boxwood, finding that as long as the bottom is flat, it will stay in the chuck.

2. Part off the top. The object here is to keep the kerf as thin as possible so that the grain will match up on the finished box.

3, 4. Hollow the box with the ¼" gouge. You could use a Jacobs chuck to drill it out, except that by the time that you find your bit, mount it in the Jacobs chuck, and put it in the tail stock, you could have already finished doing it with the gouge.

5. True up the walls and bottom with a flat scraper.

6. Cut the tenon to fit into a mortise to be cut in the lid.

7. Mount the lid in the chuck and true up the face.

8. Use a ⅟₂₀" parting tool to cut the mortise to match the tenon on the base.

9. Mount the base back into the chuck, and put the box together for any final sanding. (Boxwood should require only a light finish sanding or a Scotch Brite pad.)

10. With masking tape holding both parts together, use a small gouge to shape the top surface of the box.

11. Boxwood requires little in the way of a finish. Here, I am using wax applied with a fine Scotch-Brite pad.

12. Put a waste plug into a chuck that has been turned to the same diameter as the interior of the box, and then mount the base of the box on it.

13. Turn the bottom surface of the box. In this case, I am turning a mirror image of the top. Once the bottom has been turned, wax it the same way as you did the top.

A selection of boxes from the studio of Craig Lossing, 2" to 4" high, and 2" wide. From left to right: tulipwood with African blackwood lid; snakewood with African blackwood lid; briar burl with African blackwood lid; kingwood with African blackwood lid; and African blackwood.

(Photo by Craig Lossing)

William R. Duce, Ring boxes; African blackwood; big leaf maple burl and rosewood.

(Photo by Peter Stevens)

CLOSED VESSELS

William R. Duce, closed vessels; box elder burl with African blackwood, and poplar burl with African blackwood.

(Photo by Peter Stevens)

Closed vessels come in all shapes, sizes, and forms. The apparent simplicity of these forms provides the ideal foil to display the natural qualities found in any one piece of wood. The immediate problem that we are faced with when turning these vessels is hollowing out the waste wood from the interior of the form. For this, the scraper is a necessity.

This project features a 3" by 1¾" piece of box elder burl, with an inlay of ebony around the inside rim of the top. Placing a contrasting wood into the rim of a turning serves two purposes: first, the contrast will add visual interest; and second, it will make it seem as though you have excavated the vessel through a smaller hole than you really did.

1. Rough-turn the blank, and finish with a skew so that you will be able to judge the grain of the wood.

2. Using a ¼" skew, cut the dovetail to fit in the contracting jaws of your chuck.

3. Partially part the blank.

4. On a blank of this size, you should use a Dozuki saw to finish cutting the blank.

5. With the project piece mounted in the chuck, and the tail stock brought up for support, turn the exterior to the desired shape.

6. Move the tail stock out of the way, and shape the top however you desire.

7. Drill the piece just a little shy of the finished depth.

8. Using a variety of straight and curved scrapers, gradually work away at excavating the interior of the vessel down to the desired thickness.

9a, 9b. Use a depth gauge and thickness calipers to check your progress frequently. You will be turning blind, and all that you have to go by is the feel and sound of the tool as it turns.

Prepare an ebony plug to be glued into the hole in the top of the vessel. You can either pre-turn the plug to a finished size or glue it in and then turn it.

The method you use will depend on the wall thickness of the vessel. The walls on this one are between $1/16"$ and $3/32"$, which is fairly substantial for this type of vessel. If your walls are thinner, the stress of turning the ebony can damage your work.

10. Use cyanoacrylate to glue the ebony into the box elder.

11. Bring the tail stock up lightly to clamp it while it dries.

12a, 12b, 12c. Turn the plug down
to size and part the vessel off.

William R. Duce,
"Vessel";
box elder and
African blackwood,
2¾" high
by 2" diameter.

(Photo by Peter Stevens)

CHESSMEN

**French style chessmen,
African blackwood.**

(Photo by Peter Stevens)

The first thing I wanted to create after purchasing my lathe was a set of chessmen . . . but it didn't quite work out that way. Turning a set of chessmen is more difficult than most turners realize, but so doing is still within the skill level of the average turner. The trick is not in turning any one piece, but in turning six separate ones that share the same characteristics, so as to be identifiably from the same set. Turning a single pawn is simple enough, but creating sixteen alike is going to take a little practice.

The other problem that deters many turners is carving the knights. The Staunton style of chessmen is the most immediately identifiable style in use. But, as any collector can tell you, it is only one of a hundred that has been used down through the ages. While there are several purely turned sets which you can replicate if you so desire, do not discount the option of designing one of your own.

I have illustrated, on the opposite page, a style which I have adapted from the 1782 French *Encyclopédie*. It is not a precise copy, but is hopefully close enough to be recognizable. Finally, I have made one other deviation from the standard method of this style of turning. Traditionally, this piece would have been turned in two or three separate parts, which would have then been chased and threaded together. Doing it all in one avoids the chasing (which is cutting the threads in the wood by hand while it turns on the lathe, something I do not want to get into here), but makes it a little tight reaching into some of the corners.

(Drawing is done to life size, on a quarter-inch grid.) eightteenth-century French-styled chessmen. Left to right: king, queen, bishop, knight, rook, pawn.

The wood I am using is cherry or, as they would say on the European continent, a fruitwood.

1. Create a cardboard template outlining the form and proportions of the piece; then transfer your marks to the blank that is mounted in a screw chuck.

2. Part down to the second-widest proportion from the high point of the piece.

3. Cut away all of the extra wood on the top shaft of the piece and then reapply your lines. Notice in the photo that I have used a rare-earth magnet (nickel-plated neodymium) to hold the template in place on the tail stock.

4. Use a skew, gouge, and parting tools to form the upper part of the piece.

5. Start to shape the base with a gouge.

6. Refine the base using the point tool. The point tool is the natural instrument for this type of turning.

7. Use a fine parting tool to undercut the disk on the base.

8. Sand any rough areas.

9. Burnish with a Scotch Brite pad (you could also use steel wool).

10. Apply a wax finish.

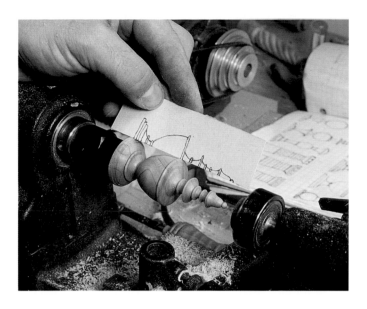

11. The completed product compared to the original template.

"Whenever I make a notable chess set I always make six extra pieces for two reasons: One, I don't like parting with my special creations; and two, I can repeat them if necessary. Even the rattle is a spare because you have to make two to get one really good one."
—Bill Jones

A. W. "Bill" Jones, Spanish Pulpit type design.
(Photo by Tony Boase)

Michael D. Mode,
"Miniature Chess Set,"
bubiniga, purpleheart,
ebony, holly, Indian
rosewood, Tagua nut,
4" diameter by 7 " high
(largest vessel).

(Photo by Bob Barrett)

GALLERY

*David Sengel, "Box,"
6" high by 3" wide,
cherry, rose thorns,
black lacquer.*

(Photo by Michael Siede)

This gallery is composed of turnings from ten of the finest contemporary turners from around the globe. The basic criteria that I used in selecting these individuals was to include only those whose work exhibits a mature sense of design, superlative craftsmanship, and a distinct sense of individual expression. In addition to this, I've only included those artisans I consider to be a continual source of inspiration for my own personal trials at the lathe.

I found that most of the turners represented in the gallery have the following traits in common:

1. They are almost all self-taught.

2. Most are professional turners, meaning that they rely on the sales of their turnings as their major source of income.

3. They all share in a true passion for working with wood.

4. Woodturning is a second (or third) career for most.

5. And they are all some of the nicest people that you could ever hope to meet.

KIP CHRISTENSEN

An Associate Professor of Technology Education at Brigham Young University, Kip shares his passion for working with wood with teaching furniture design and construction (in addition to other courses). A champion of the small-scale object, Kip has pioneered the use of elk and moose antler as a serious material for artistic turning.

"Lidded Container,"
pink ivory, ebony, bone,
elk antler, 3⅝" high by
1⅞" diameter.

(Photos by Photocraft, Orem, UT)

"Lidded Jewelry Bowl,"
elk antler, ebony,
turquoise, 1¾" high by
3⅝" diameter.

DAVID ELLSWORTH

David Ellsworth is a name that any turner is sure to recognize. A leader in the contemporary turning field, David has elevated the level of awareness of woodturning to a fine art form with both his large- and small-scale work. A gifted teacher, he continues to inspire countless others to take to their shop and straddle their lathes.

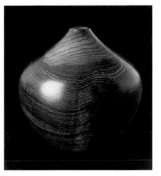

"Kingwood Vessel,"
3½" by 3".

"Three Vessels,"
cocobolo/rosewood
burl, tallest 1⅜".

"Salt & Pepper
Shakers,"
cocobolo/rosewood,
2¾".

A. W. JONES

*"Copenhagen/Tulip
Chess Patterns," ivory;
Bill counts this as his
finest achievement of
work and design.*

(Photos by Tony Boase)

At seventy-eight years young, Bill Jones is a fifth-generation English hardwood and ivory turner. The requirements of Bill's style of work demand precise hand screw cutting and spindle carving. He has written a regular column in *Woodturning* since it's inception, and the magazine's first forty articles are covered in his two books, *Bill Jone's Notes from the Turning Shop* and *Further Notes from the Turning Shop*.

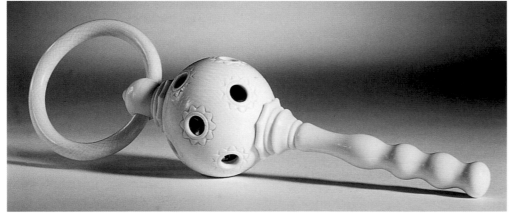

*"Ornamental Ivory
Rattle (with Silver
Bells)," commissioned
by the Worshipful Co.
of Turners for Princess
Diana's First Born.*

BONNIE KLEIN

As the dynamo behind Klein Design Inc., Bonnie has designed the Klein Woodturning Lathe, as well as a complete line of accessories and videos geared towards the small-scale turner. Bonnie is an internationally recognized demonstrator, teacher, and turner of small-scale objects whose name is synonymous with this style of turning.

"Threaded Box," mopane, African blackwood, bone.

"Top Boxes," African blackwood, Osage orange.

"Chess Set," African blackwood and boxwood.

MICHAEL LEE

Mike Lee has certainly come a long way since his initial turning attempts resulted, as he puts it, in the "fine art of bludgeoning wood." Now a full-time studio turner, Mike's work unequivocally captures the energy and vitality of his Hawaiian surroundings.

"Crater Pod," milo, 5½" diameter by 6" high.

(Photo by Hugo de Vries)

"Space Pod," maple burl, 3½" diameter by 3" high.

"Rock-A-Bye Pod," eucalyptus burl, 5¾" long by 3" wide by 3" high. (Photo by Hugo de Vries)

CRAIG LOSSING

Like many of us, Craig is a self-taught artisan. Now a full-time studio turner, Craig has adapted his lifelong pursuit of art to creating exquisite containers that reflect his passion for the medium and his mastery of design. As a sideline, Craig also retails some of the wonderful wood that he features in his work

Panamanian cocobolo,
4" by 4".

(Photos by Craig Lossing)

Ebony, maple burl,
bloodwood, 7" high by
12" wide.

Maple, ebony, plywood,
6" high by 9" wide.

MICHAEL D. MODE

A full-time studio turner, Michael's work expresses his passion for the art and architecture of Mughal India and the Islamic world, which he acquired during his extensive travels through the Middle East and Kashmir

Michael D. Mode, "Miniature Chess Set," bubiniga, purpleheart, ebony, holly, Indian rosewood, Tagua nut, 4" diameter by 7½" high (largest vessel).

(Photos by Bob Barrett)

"Miniature Chess Set," Indian rosewood, holly, ebony, Tagua nut, 5½" diameter by 5¾" high (with lid on).

DAVID SENGEL

Tiring of the long-term commitments that come with a career repairing grand pianos, David found the immediacy that he craved at the lathe. A full-time studio turner, David is best known for his turnings that feature ebonizing, thorns, sandblasting, and multi-axis turning, but he still professes a love for the simple and unadorned natural material.

"Box," cherry, rose thorns, crab claws, black lacquer, 3" high by 3" wide.

"Box," mulberry, rose, and locust thorns, black lacquer, 6" high by 4" wide.

(Photos by Michael Siede)

"Teacup and Saucer," pearwood, rose thorns, black lacquer, 4" high by 5" wide.

HANS J. WEISSFLOG

"Star Box," African blackwood, 1⅞" by 2⅞".

(Photos by Hans J. Weissflog)

Hans Weissflog has taken the motto "*Klein und Fein*" ("small and fine"), and made it his own. Internationally known for his "Ball Box, turned broken through," this master of the form continues to press the limits of the craft and delight and amaze turners everywhere.

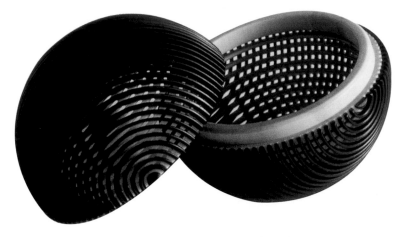

"Ball Box, turned broken through," African blackwood/ boxwood, 2".

"Round-Square-Oval Box," African blackwood/box-wood, 2" by 2⅜".

MOHAMED ZAKARIYA

Mohamed is a true Renaissance man. A leading authority on Islamic calligraphy, Mohamed has exhibited, studied, and taught calligraphy all around the world. Utilizing his skills as a machinist, engraver, and turner, he also re-creates precise antique-styled scientific and horological instruments, including thirteen functioning astrolabes.

"Short Vessel," boxwood, 7¾". (Photos by Samuel Gutterman)

"Short Vessel," box-wood, 7¾"

"Cylindrical Sundial," boxwood and steel, 7" high.

TURNING RESOURCES

I believe that the greatest resource for any small-scale turner is the American Association of Woodturners. This organization is composed of individuals just like you, and the wealth of knowledge that is to be found in its journal, videos, and special publications is second to none.

American Association of Woodturners

3200 Lexington Ave.
Shoreview, MN 55126
612-484-9094

One other resource that should not be overlooked is the Internet. By typing in a few key words, there is a world of information that awaits you. Enjoy.

Index